Gastronomic
DICTIONARY

Portuguese - English

Thomas Harmsworth

Thomas Harmsworth's

Gastronomic Dictionary

Portuguese-English

THOMAS HARMSWORTH PUBLISHING COMPANY

First Published 2008

Thomas Harmsworth Publishing Company

Old Rectory Offices

Stoke Abbott

Beaminster DT8 3JT.

British Library Cataloguing-in-Publication Data. A catalogue record of this book is available from the British Library.

In the same series:
French-English
Spanish-English
Italian-English

ISBN 978-0-948807-61-9

ISSN 1741-3370

Printed in Great Britain by

Remous Limited

Introduction

Gastronomic Dictionary is designed to enable the diner to make sense of menus written in Portuguese. It covers many of the questions a traveller might ask a waiter in a restaurant. It also enables the diner to select a restaurant by reading menus first, and choosing one according to what one fancies at the time. Several restaurants may be equally good, but according to one's mood, one menu may appeal more than another at any particular moment! *Gastronomic Dictionary* may also prove useful to Portuguese waiters with english-speaking customers; and to cookery students.

Portuguese is a very large language. It has three times as many words as Spanish. It is in current use in four continents, has many regional words, and is a language which is prone to short-lived fashionable additions.

The dictionary not only covers Portugal itself, but also, largely, Brazil. There are other Portuguese speaking-countries. These include Angola, Mozambique, Guinea-Bissau, the Cape Verde Islands, and São Tomé and Principe. Restaurants in these African territories offer menus very similar to those in Portugal; although the dishes are influenced by local ingredients. This means that pineapple, coconut and fish may well feature more often here than in Portugal itself.

Brazil is the largest country in South America, and the only one that speaks Portuguese (all the rest are Spanish-speaking). Here, the Amazon basin and coastline are rich in fish, many of them little known to the english palate.

The definitions are not intended to describe every aspect of a dish, but just enough of the basic ingredients to indicate its character; and it does not cover specialist restaurants (e.g. Chinese).

Gastronomic Dictionary also covers many kitchen implements and receptacles. This is because dishes are often described by the pots they are cooked in. For the same reason a few wines are included. And because travelling involves accommodation, a few hotel terms, car parking terms &c feature among the definitions.

There are quite a few words in English for which there is no succinct Portuguese synonym. This results in the translation consisting of a long string of descriptive words. For instance, 'honeydew melon' translates to the equivalent of 'variety of melon with a very sweet pale-green flesh.' If individual words in such a string appear on their own in the menu, they will be found in *Gastronomic Dictionary;* but no attempt has been made to incorporate whole strings of words, because these may vary according to the compiler of the menu.

Let us know what additions you can contribute (and in the same format with gender, applicable regions &c as in *Gastronomic Dictionary).*

A

abacate *nm* avocado pear
abacaxi *nm* pineapple
abafador *nm* (of teapot) cosy
abancar *vt* to seat at table at a bench
abandejado *a* tray-like
abandejar *vt* to make tray-shaped
abano *nm* (of fruit) windfall, ripe fruit
abarana (uborana) (ubarana) *nf* [Braz] sea fish: ladyfish
abarrotar *vt* to cram
abartar *vt* (of price) to undercut, to cheapen
abastamento *nm* abundance, glut
abastança *nf* abundance, glut
abastar *vt* to supply, to cater
abastecimento *nm* provisioning
abastoso *a* abundant
abatatar *vt* to shape potato-like
abatedouro *nm* slaughter house, abattoir
abater *vt* (of price) to discount, to reduce; (of cattle) to slaughter; *vi* (of soufflé) to collapse
abatido *a* (of price) reduced; (of cattle) slaughtered
abatimento *nm* (of money) discount
abatis *nm* (of fowl) giblets
abatumado *a* (of meat) tough; (of bread &c) stodgy
abeberado *a* (of thirst) quenched, slaked
abeberar *vt* to drink; **~-se** *vi* to drink; to soak up
abelha *nf* honey bee
abelheira *nf* beehive
abelheiro *nm* bee-keeper
aberém *nm* maize or rice-flour cake
abetarda *nf* bustard; large game bird
abetumado *a* (of bread &c) stodgy
abiaxar *vt* (of dough) to beat
abiscoitado *a* biscuit/cracker-like
abiscoitar *vt* to bake like a biscuit
abluir *vt* (of hands &c) to wash
abóbora *nf* pumpkin; marrow; **~-d'água (abobrinha)** summer squash; **~-carneira** calabash; **~-menina** giant gourd; winter squash **~-porqueira** melon pumpkin
abobrinha *nf* courgette, zucchini; **(abóbora-d'água)** summer squash
abocanhar (aboquejar) *vt* to bite, to bite off
abolachado *a* biscuit/cracker-like
abolachar *vt* to bake like a biscuit
abolado *a* cake-like
abotoado (cuiu-cuiu) (armado) (armao) *nm* freshwater catfish

abrasamento *nm* fire
abrasar *vt/vi* to burn, to singe, to overheat
abraseado (esbraseado) *a* (of embers &c) glowing
abrasear (esbrasear) *vt* to heat to glowing
abre (cachaça) *nm* brandy
abricó (abricote) *nm* apricot
abrideira *nf* brandy
abril *nm* April
abrir *vt* (of bottle/door/oyster &c) to open; to make an incision; **~ o apetite** (of appetite) to whet, to sharpen; **~ peixe** (of fish) to gut
abrótea *nf* sea fish: ling; hake
abrunheiro *nm* (of tree) damson
abrunho *nm* (of tree) sloe
absinto *nm* (of liqueur) absinthe
absorvente *a* (of paper &c) absorbent
absorver *vt* to swallow; to drink; to absorb
abstemia *nf* abstemiousness
abstêmio *a* teetotal; abstemious; *nm* teetotaller
abstenção *nf* abstinence; fast
abstinência *nf* abstinence; sobriety; fast
abstinente *nm/f* abstainer
abundância *nf* abundance, plenty, glut
abundante *a* abundant, plentiful; **~mente** abundantly
abundar *vi* to abound (in)
abusar *vt* (of alcohol) to abuse
abuso *nm* abuse
acabaçado *a* (of shape/taste &c) gourd-like
acabaçar *vt* to shape gourd-like
acabar *vt* to finish, to end; **acabando** (of supplies) running-out
acaçá *nm* [Braz] maize/rice cake; fermented maize/rice drink
açaflor (açafrão) *nm* saffron
açafroa *nf* safflower
açafroado *a* flavoured with saffron
açafroar *vt* to flavour with saffron
acaju *nm* cashew nut
acamar *vt* to layer
acanelar *vt* to cinnamon
acapno *a* honey obtained without smoking the bees out
acará *nm* [Braz] beans/palm oil dish; **~-açu** [Braz] freshwater fish: oscar; **~-bandeira** [Braz] freshwater fish: angel-fish; scalare
acarajé *nm* dendê palm oil-fried kidney bean paste
acastelado *a* (of cake decoration &c) castellated
acavalar *vt* to layer overlapping
acebolado *a* onions-covered; onions-influenced
acebolar *vt* (of dish) to cover with onions; to introduce onions
acelga *nf* Swiss Chard

acém *nm* (of meat) fore-rib, chuck rib
acendedor *nm* (of cigarettes &c) lighter
acender *vt* to light, to ignite; *vi* to catch fire; **~ a luz** (of lamp) to switch on
acentor *nm* sparrow
acepipe *nm* tit-bit; delicacy; **~s de mariscos** seafood cocktail
acepipeiro *nm* (of person) sweet tooth
aceragem *nf* cutlery; sharpening
acerar *vt* to sharpen
acerejar *vt* (of meat &c) to sear
acérrimo *a* (of taste) very bitter
acervejado *a* beer-tasting
acetinado *a* (of paper) tissue
acetoso *a* vinegary
acevadar *vt* barley-feed
acevar *vt* to fatten-up
achar *nm* pickled fruit/herbs/ roots
acidez *nf* acidity, sourness
acidificar (acidular) *vt* to add vinegar/lemon &c
ácido *nm/a* acid; **~ tartárico** tartaric acid
acidrado *a* citron-like
acídulo *a* (of wine) acidulous
acima *adv* above
acincho *nm* cheese press, cheese mould
aço *nm* [Braz] white rum (slang)
acola *nf* chocolate/maize-flour titbit
acomodação *nf* accommodation; room; lodging
acomodar *vt* (of B&B) to accommodate; to retire to one's room
acompanhado (por) *a* (of dish) accompanied (by)
acompanhamento *nm* accompaniment; side-dish; dressing
acompanhar *vt* (of dish) to serve with
aconchego *nm* lodging; comfort
aconfeitado *a* like confectionery
aconfeitar *vt* to make like confectionery
açorda *nf* panada; bread soup
açoteado *a* (of restaurant) terrace
açougue *nm* butcher's; abattoir
açougueiro *nm* butcher
acre *a* tart; **~-doce** sweet and sour
acresentar *vt* (of dish) to stretch
acridiano (acrídio) *nm* locust
actínia *nf* sea anemone
açu *a* [Braz] large
açúcar *nm* sugar; **~ areado** icing-sugar; **~ de beterraba** beet sugar; **camada de ~ (cobertura de ~)** icing; **~ de cana** cane sugar; **~-cande** (of confectionery) sugar-candy; sweet; candy [USA]; **coberto de ~** sugar-coated,

crystallised sugar; **~ cristal** granulated sugar; **~ dos diabéticos** saccharin(e); **~ mascavo** brown-sugar; **pão de ~** sugar loaf; **~ pilé** crushed sugar; granulated sugar; **~ em pó** icing sugar; **~ em rama** raw sugar; **~ refinado** castor sugar; loaf-sugar; **~ em tabletes (torrão de ~)** cube sugar, lump sugar

açucarado *a* sweet; sugary

açucarar *vt* to sweeten; to sugar

açucareiro *nm* sugar bowl

açucena *nf* [Braz] candlestick socket/holder

adagueiro *nm* young stag

adamascado *a* apricot-tasting

adega *nf* wine-cellar, cellar

adegar *vt* (of wine) to keep (in cellar)

adegueiro *nm* cellarman; butler

adeus! *nm* goodbye!

adeusinho *interj* cheerio!

adiantar *vt* to pre-pay

adição *nf* (of restaurant) bill

adicionado *a* added

adicionador *nm* adding machine

adicional *nm/nf* supplement, extra; *a* extra, supplementary; **pagamento ~** (of payment) supplementary

adicionar *vt* to add

adietar *vi* to diet

aditivo *nm* additive

ado *nm* dendê oil-toasted maize

adoçado *a* sugared, sweetened

adoçamento *nm* sweetening

adoçar *vt* to sweeten

adocicado *a* sweetened; sweetish

adocicar *vt* to sweeten

adstringência *nf* (of wine) tartness

adubar *vt* to season, to flavour

adubo *nm* seasoning, flavouring; spices

adufa *nf* olive oil-press crusher

adulçorar *vt* to sweeten, to soften

adulterar *vt* to adulterate

aeroporto *nm* airport

afatiar *vt* to slice

aferventação *nf* par-boiling

aferventado *nm* par-boiled

afiado *a* sharpened

afiador *nm* (of knife) grinder

afiambrar *vt* (of meat) to cure; to pickle

afiar *vt* (of knife) to sharpen; to grind

afrodisíaco *nm* aphrodisiac

afrutado *a* fruited

afrutar *vi* to fruit

afumado (defumado) (esfumado) *a* smoked, cured

afumadura *nf* smoking

afumar *vt* to smoke

afurá *nf* fermented rice drink

ágape *nm* banquet

ágar-ágar *nm* agar-agar

agárico *nm* (of mushroom)

agaric

agave *nf* agave, tequila-producing plant

agente de conservação de alimentos *nm/f* food preservative

agitar *vt* to shake

agosto *nm* August

agraço *nm* verjuice; unripe grape

agre (acre) (agro) *a* bitter; sour

agregado *nm* [Braz] houseman (servant)

agregar *vt* to add

agremiação *nf* reunion

agreste *a* wild

agrião *nm* watercress

agridoce *a* bitter sweet

agro (acre) (agre) *a* bitter, sour

agrumelar (agrumular) *vi* to thicken

água *nf* water, river, lake, sea; **~s** spa; **~-de-briga** [Braz] rum; **~ de chuva** rainwater; **~-de-coco** coconut milk; **~ doce** fresh water, freshwater, sweet water; **~ férrea** mineral water, spring, chalybeate; **~ com gas** fizzy water; **~ sem gas** still water; **~ gasosa** sparkling water; **~ gelada** ice, iced water; **~-mel** mead, honey and water; **~ mineral** mineral water; **~ que passarinho não bebe** brandy, rum; **~ salgada** salt water; **~-só** (of game bird) snipe; **~ termal** hot spring; **~ de torneira** tap water; **~ viva** running water

aguadeiro *nm* water-seller

aguado *a* [Braz] (of tea/coffee &c) with sugar; watery

aguapé *nf* light wine

aguar *vt* to dilute; to add water

aguardentado *a* brandied

aguardentar *vt* to brandy

aguardente *nf* brandy; marc; brandy spirits; **~ de cana-de-açúcar (cachaça)** high alcohol rum; **~ de cereais** whisky; corn-brandy; **~ escandinava** aquavit; **~ de frutas** brandy; **~ de maçãs** marc; **~ ordinária** strong liquor; **~ oriental** arrack; **~ de uvas** brandy; marc

aguçado *a* (of knife) sharp, sharpened

aguçador *nm* (of knife) sharpener, grinder

aguçadura *nf* (of knife) sharpening, grinding

aguçar *vt* (of knife) to sharpen, to grind

agulha *nf* (of beef &c) shoulder; (of sewing) needle; (of wine) sharpness; sea fish: needle fish, horn fish

agulhão *nm* [Braz] sea fish: needlefish; **~-bandeira (~-vela)** sea fish: atlantic sailfish

agutiguepe ([Braz] **araruta)** *nf* arrowroot

aia *nf* chambermaid
aiaçá *nf* [Braz] freshwater turtle
aipi (aipim) ([Braz] **macaxeira, mandioca-doce, uaipi)** *nm* sweet cassava
aipo *nm* celery; **~-do-banhado** (of red food colouring) amaranth; **~-rábano** celeriac
aivão *nm* pheasant
ajantarado *nm* main Sunday meal
ajudante de cozinha *nm/f* kitchen boy/maid
alabote (halabote) *nm* sea fish: halibut
alagostado *a* lobster coloured
alambiqueiro *nm* (of person) distiller
alanhar *vt* (of fish) to gut, to clean
alaranjado *a* orange-ed
alardar *vt* to lard
alares *nm* (of bird-trapping) net
alarvaria *nf* gluttony
albacora *nf* sea fish: tuna, tunny
albardar *vt* (of baking) to crumb; to batter
albarrã *nf* wild onion
albarrada *nf* mug
albergador *nm* (of reception) host
albergamento *nm* lodging
albergar *vt/vi* to lodge
albergaria (albergue *nm) nf* inn, tavern
albergueiro *nm* innkeeper
alboroque *nm* (of agreement-signing) celebratory meal
albragar *vt* to bread
albricoque *nm* apricot
albufeira *nf* olive (remaining) water
albume (albúmen) (albumina *nf) nm* egg-white
alcachofra *nf* artichoke
alcaçuz *nm* liquorice (licorice)
alcadafe (alcadefe) *nm* pub spirit measure; pub overspill receptacle
álcali *nm* alkali
alcamonia *nf* cassava-flour/honey sweet (candy)
alcaparra *nf* caper
alcaparrado *a* caper-ed
alcaparreira-cheirosa *nf* mustard shrub
alcaravia *nf* (of cakes &c) caraway seed
alcatira *nf* (of food additive) tragacanth
alcatra *nf* (of beef) rump
alce *nm* moose, elk
álcool *nm* alcohol; spirits; **sem ~** non-alcoholic
alcoólico *a* alcoholic; **não ~** non-alcoholic
álcoolização *nf* distillation
alcorça *nf* (of sugar) icing
aldeão *a* rural, rustic
alecrim *nm* rosemary; **~-do-norte** (of brewing) bog myrtle
alegre *a* happy; cheerful; slightly tipsy
aleijada *nf* sugar cane variety
aleitativo *a* (of pig) suckling

alentado *a* juicy, succulent
alentador *a* nourishing
alentar *vt* to nourish
Alentejo *nm* wine-growing region; **evora de l'~** hard goat cheese
alento *nm* nourishment, food
alergênio *nm* allergen
alergia *nf* allergy
alérgico *a* allergic
aletria *nf* vermicelli
aletriado *a* vermicelli-like
álevedar *vt* to leaven; to ferment
alevim *nm* (of young fish) fry
alfabeto *nm* (of pasta &c) alphabet
alface *nf* lettuce; **~ repolhuda** cabbage lettuce
alfafa (luzerna) *nf* alfalfa
alfaia *nf* tableware; silver tray; domestic implement
alfandegário *a* customs; **sob guarda ~a** (of goods) in bond
alfarroba *nf* carob, locust bean
alfavaca *nf* basil; **~-cheirosa** sweet basil; **~-de-cobra** (of herb) feverfew
alfazema *nf* lavender
alféloa *nf* icing; confectionery
alfeloeiro *nm* confectioner
alfênico *nm* cane sugar
alfenim *nm* confectionery
alfitete *nm* large pie; large pastry; sweet dough; baconed sweet dough
alfonsia (alforra) *nf* mildew
alforjada *nf* bagful
alforjar *vt* to bag
alga *nf* seaweed
algodão-doce *nm* (of confectionery) candy-floss
alguidar *nm* earthenware bowl; metal bowl
alhada *nf* garlic; garlic-ed stew
alhal *nm* in-kitchen firewood store
alheira *nf* (of vegetable) yellow rocket; spiced pork/chicken sausage
alheiro *nm* garlic seller
alho *nm* garlic; **dente de ~** garlic clove; **~ porro (~ poró)** leek
aligátor *nm* alligator
alimentação *nf* alimentation, nourishment; **~ equilibrada** balanced diet
alimentar *vt* alimentary, nourishing
alimentício *a* alimentary, nourishing
alimento *nm* food
alimentoso *a* alimentary, nourishing
alismatácea *nf* plantain
almadrava *nf* tunny fishing
almalho *nm* bullock
almeirão *nm* wild chicory
almiscareiro *nm* musk-deer
almoçadeira *nf* large cup
almoçar *vi* to breakfast; to lunch
almoço *nm* breakfast; lunch
almofariz *nm* pestle; mortar
almofeira *nf* olive water

almojávena *nf* small cheese tart
almôndega *nf* meatball; hamburger; **~ de peixe** fishball
alô *interject* hello!
aloirado *a* (of wine colour) golden; **~ claro** (of wine colour) light-gold
alosna (losna) *nf* (of herb) wormwood
alourar *vt/vi* to brown; (of meat-cooking &c) to seal-in the juices
alpaca *nf* alpaca
alperche (alperce) *nm* large apricot
altéia *nf* (of herb) marshmallow
alto-mar *nm* deep sea, open sea
altor (altriz) *a* nutritive
aluá *nm* fermented rice flour/ maize
alumínio *nm* aluminium
alva *nf* grape variety
alvaçâo *a* (of cattle) white variety
alvarinho *nm* grape variety
alveário *nm* bee hive
alvéolo *nm* honeycomb cell; (of seed) pod
alverca *nm* semi-hard ewe or goat cheese
alvergue *nm* olive press tank
alvissareiro *nm* (of gratuities) tipper
Alvito *nm* Alentejo vineyard
alvo *nm* white; clear; pure
alvor *nm* whiteness
amadurado (maduro) *a* ripe
amaduramento *nm* ripeness; ripening
amadurar (amadurecer) *vi* to ripen; to mature
amadurecido (maduro) (amadurado) *a* ripe; mature
amalgamar *vt* to amalgamate; to mix-in
amanhã *adv* tomorrow; **depois de ~** the day after tomorrow
amanhação *nf* (of land) cultivation; dressing; preparing
amanhado *nm* dressed fish &c
amanhador *nm* (of food) dresser; preparer; cook
amanhar *vt* (of meat/fish &c) to prepare; to gut; to clean
amanhecido *a* (of bread &c) stale; old
amanteigado *nm* [Braz] egg/ flour cake
amanteigar *vt* to butter; to make buttery
amáraco *nm* (of herb) sweet marjoram
amarelo *nm* unpasteurized ewe's milk cheese
amargo *nm* bitter; [Braz] (of tea &c) without sugar
amargor *nm* bitter taste
amarguinha *nf* sour-almond liqueur
amarugem *nm* slightly bitter taste
amarujar *vi* to taste slightly bitter

amarujento *a* bitter-tasting
amarulento *a* bitter
amarume *nm* bitterness
amassadeira *nf* (of person) kneader
amassadela *nf* kneading
amassado *a* flattened, squashed, crushed
amassador *nm* kneading trough
amassadouro *nm* kneading trough, kneading board
amassadura *nf* kneading
amassar *vt* to knead; to mix
amassaria *nf* kneading trough; bakery
amassilho *nm* flour for kneading
ambiente *nm* (of restaurant) ambience
amboré *nm* [Braz] sea fish: scorpion fish
ambrósia *nf* ambrosia; food of the gods; [Braz] egg/sugar/milk confectionery; egg custard
ambrosíaco *a* delicious
ambulância *nf* ambulance
amealhar *vi* to haggle; to economise
amêijoa *nf* cockle; clam
ameijoada *nf* cockle stew
ameixa (amêixla) *nf* plum; **~ seca** prune; **~s cozidas** stewed prunes
amelaçar *vi* to make syrup/ molasses
ameloado *a* melon-tasting/ shaped/coloured
amêndoa *nf* almond; Easter present; kernel-ed nut
amendoada *nf* orgeat; almond syrup; almond cake
amendoado *a* almond-ed
amendoim *nm* peanut, groundnut; **manteiga-de-~** peanut butter
ameno *a* delicious
americano *a* American; **à ~** (of dish) shellfished tomatoed flambé-ed
amido *nm* starch
amilhado *a* (of animal) maize/ corn-fed
amilhar *vt/vi* to feed with maize/ corn; (of dish) to maize-include
amoladeira *nf* grindstone
amolado *a* sharpened
amolador *nm* (of knife) sharpener; grinder
amolar *vt* (of knife) to sharpen; to grind
amoldar *vt* to mould
amor-crescido *nm* sunflower
amora *nf* mulberry; **~-preta** blackberry
amorsegar *vt* to bite off
amostado *a* must (unfermented grapejuice)-tasting
amostardado *a* mustard-included
amostra *nf* sample; **~ grátis** free sample
ampelológico *a* vineyard-cultivation
anabás *nm* freshwater fish:

anabas; perch
anáfega (jujuba) *nf* jujube fruit
analgésico *a* analgesic
analuri *nf* Amazon turtle variety
ananás (ananaseiro) *nm* (of plant) pineapple
anar *vt* (of fire &c) to fan, to fan-cool
anatado *a* creamy
anatar *vt* to cream
anatídeos *nm* anatidae; waterfowl family (eg ducks/ geese)
anatifa *nf* acorn barnacle
anavalhado *a* sharp
anca *nf* hindquarters; haunch
anchova (enchova) *nf* anchovy; bluefish
andar *nm* (of building) storey, floor; **andar térreo** ground floor
andino *a* Andean
andu *nm* pigeon pea; seed of cajan
anel (anéis *pl) nm* (of cooker &c) ring; **~éis de lula à doré** battered squid rings
anêmona-do-mar *nf* sea anemone
aneto *nm* dill
aneurina *nf* vitamin B
angélica *nf* angelica
ânglico *a* English
angolinha *nf* [Braz] guinea-fowl
angu *nm* boiled maize; boiled manioc flour
angüite *nf* [Braz] (of dish) shrimps/fish/pepper/oil/herbs
angula *nf* sea fish: elver
angustura *nf* angostura
anguzô *nm* angu/angüite mix
anielado *a* enamelled
anis *nm* aniseed; **~ -doce** fennel; **~-estrelado** star anise
anisar *vt* to aniseed-flavour
aniseta (anisete *nm) nf* (of liqueur) anisette
aniversário *nm* birthday; anniversary; **~ de casamento** wedding anniversary
ano *nm* year; birthday; **quadra do ~** (of the year) season
anonácea *nf* custard apple variety
anonário *a* food
anorgânico *a* inorganic
antena *nf* tentacle
antepagar *vt* to pay up front
antepasto *nm* starters; antipasto; hors d'oeuvre
antiácido *nm* antacid
antílope *nm* antelope
anujá *nf* [Braz] freshwater catfish
anulação *nf* (of table reservation) cancellation
apagador *nm* (of candle) snuffer; extinguisher
apagar *vt/vi* (of candle) to snuff out; to extinguish; (of thirst) to quench
apaiari *nm* [Braz] freshwater fish: oscar
apaladar *vt* (of flavour) to

enhance
apanhadeira *nf* (of person) fruit picker; gleaner
apapá (sardinhão) (dorada) *nm* [Braz] freshwater fish: Amazonion herring
aparadeira *nf* drip-tray
aparador *nm* dumb-waiter
aparar *vt* (of meat &c) to trim; to trim-off
aparelho *nm* equipment; apparatus; basic-ingredients mixture/base; ~ **de chá** tea service
apartamento *nm* (of accommodation) flat
apelido *nm* surname
aperiente (aperitivo) *a* aperitif
aperitivo *nm/a* aperitif; appetizer
apertar *vt* to squeeze; to press
apetecedor *a* appetizing
apetência (apetite) *nf* appetite
apetente *a* appetizing
apetisoso *a* appetizing; salty
apetite *nm* appetite; hunger
apiário *nm* apiary
apiastro (erva-cidreira) *nm* (of herb) lemon balm
apicultor *nm* beekeeper
apicultura *nf* beekeeping
apimentado *a* spicy; peppery; piquant; **muito** ~ devilled
apimentar *vt* to spice, to pepper, to add piquancy
apolentar *vt* (of animals) to polenta-fatten
aportuguesado *a* portuguese style
aposentar *vt* (as host) to lodge
aprazível *a* (of restaurant) with-beautiful-view
aprovisionador *nm* supplier
aprovisionamento *nm* victualling; purveying; supply
aprovisionar *vt* to victual; to purvey; to supply
apurar *vt* to cook slowly to bring out flavour; to heat; to assimilate
aquário *nm* aquarium
aquartilhar *vt* to sell/measure by the pint
aquecedor *nm* heater
aquecer *vt* to heat; to warm
aquecido *a* heated
aquecimento (central) *nm* (central) heating
aquecível *a* heatable
aquentar *vt* to heat; to warm
áqüeo *a* watery
aquiqui *nm* [Braz] inferior Indian brandy of maize
ar *nm* air; **ao ~ livre** outdoors; ~ **condicionado** air-conditioned
arabaiana (olho-de-vidro [Braz]) sea fish: amberjack
araca *nf* arrack; rice brandy; sugar-cane brandy; date brandy
araçá *nm* Brazilian guava; **~-da-praia (~s-de-coroa)** strawberry guava
araçaeiro (araçázeiro) *nm* Brazilian guava
araçaí *nm* Brazilian guava

aracangüira *nm* [Braz] sea fish: threadfish
aração *nf* gulping down
araçazada *nf* [Braz] (of confectionery) strawberry guava sweet
araçazeiro (araçareiro) *nm* [Braz] Brazilian guava
aracu-comun *nm* [Braz] freshwater fish: three-spot leporinus; aracu
arado *a* [Braz] hungry
araguaguá *nm* [Braz] sea fish: sawfish
aramaçá (aramaçã) *nm* [Braz] Amazonian flounder
arandela *nf* candlestick socket
aranha-do-mar *nf* crawfish; spider crab
araracangaçu (tracajá) *nm* freshwater turtle
araroba *nf* Goa powder
arartucupé *nf* [Braz] (of tree) nitta tree
araruta *nf* arrowroot
aratanha *nf* [Braz] a small cow
araticum *nm* (of shrub) custard-apple variety
aratu *nm* [Braz] small crab
arca *nf* box; ~ **do pão** bread-bin
ardido *a* rancid
areado *a* (of texture) sandy; (of sugar &c) dusted; **açúcar ~** icing-sugar
arear *vt* to dust; to sand
areca *nf* betal-nut
areia-preta *nf* snuff
arejar *vt* (of fruit) to wither; to go dry
arenque *nm* herring; anchovy; **~ fumado** kipper; buckling; bloater
argau *nm* (of wine) pipette
argentão *nm* German silver
argentar *vt* to silver-plate
argentaria *nf* silverware
argentário *nm* silverware cupboard
argentina *nf* (of fish) smelts
argentino *a* Argentine
argila *nf* argil; potter's earth
argola *nf* napkin ring
argolinha *nf* small biscuit; (of soup) pastry
aría *nf* [Braz] arrowroot variety
arimbá *nm* [Braz] glazed clay jar
arinca *nf* sea fish: haddock; **~ fumada** smoked haddock
arinta (arinto *nm) nf* white grape variety
armado (armao) (abotoado) (cuiu-cuiu) *nm* freshwater catfish
armarinho *nm* small cupboard
armário *nm* cupboard; **~ de cozinha** kitchen cabinet; **~ de pão** bread-bin
armazém *nm* shop; **~ de secos e molhados (mercearia)** grocery
armazenar *vt* to store; **~ em celeiro** (of wine) to lay down
armolão *nm* [Braz] spinach
aroma *nm* aroma; flavour; smell; (of wine) bouquet

aromático *a* aromatic; spicy; flavoured; **ervas ~as** herbs
aromatizador *a* flavouresome
aromatizante *a* flavouring
aromatizar *vt* to (add) flavour
arracimar-se *vi* to cluster grape-like
arraia (raia) *nf* sea fish: skate; **~-viola** sea fish: guitar-fish
arranca (arrancada) *nf* [Braz] cassava harvesting
arranca-estrepe *nm* barbifruit pavonia
arranchar *vt* (of military) to mess
arrátel *nm* 16 ounces
arratelar *vt* to sell/weigh by the pound
arredondar *vt* to make round
arrefecer *vt* to cool
arrepiar *vt* (of fish) to prepare with salt
arriba *adv* up
arribação *nf* arrival; beans/rice/pigeon-dish
arrobe *nm* [Braz] boiled wine; fruit juice; fruit syrup
arrolhador *nm* bottle corker
arrolhamento *nm* corkage
arrolhar *vt* (of bottle) to cork
arroz *nm* rice; **~-de-carreteiro** [Braz] riced beef/sausage/garlic/onion/parsley/chives dish; **~-de-cuxá** [Braz] cuxá/rice-dish, ginger/vinegar-sauced rice; **~-doce (~-de-leite)** rice-pudding, milk pudding; **~-de-festa** [Braz] (of guest) party animal; **~-de-função** [Braz] cinnamon/rice dessert; **~ integral** brown rice; **~ salvagem** wild rice
arrozalva *nf* [Braz] rice flour
arrozeiro *a* rice-loving
arrubé *nm* [Braz] cassava oil
arrumadeira *nf* [Braz] house-maid
arrumador *nm* manservant
artemísia *nf* (of spice) oriental wormwood
artéria *nf* artery
ártico *a* arctic
artófago *a* bread-eating
artólatra *nm* bread-lover
aruaná (arowana) *nm* [Braz] large Amazon freshwater fish: silver arowana
arubé ([Braz] **arubê)** *nm* cassava/garlic/pepper/salt/fish-sauce flavouring
arugula (eruca) *nf* (of herb) rocket
arumará *nm* [Braz] blackbird variety
arumarana *nf* [Braz] (of herb) alligatorflag, fireflag
árvore *nf* tree; **~-do-papel-de-arroz** (of plant) rice paper
asa *nf* (of chicken) wing; (of coffee-pot &c) handle
ascensor (elevador) *nm* lift, elevator
ascensorista *nm/f* [Braz] lift-boy
asco *nm* mushroom spore
asimina *nf* custard-apple; paw-

paw

asmo *a* (of bread) unleavened
asno *nm* donkey
aspargo *nm* asparagus
aspermo *a* seedless
áspero *a* rough; (of wine) off
aspersão *nf* sprinkling
asperso *a* sprinkled
aspirina *nf* asprin
assa-fétida *nf* (of condiments) asafoetida
assacate *nm* tallow
assadeira *nf* peanut-vendor; chesnut-vendor; roasting pan; baking pan; baking sheet
assado *nm* (of meat) roast; **~s** roast meats; *a* baked; roast; **~ demais** overdone; **pouco ~** under-done; **frango ~** roast chicken
assador (assadeiro) *nm* roaster; dutch oven; [Braz] (of roasting) spit
assadura *nf* roasting; baking; roasting meat
assalmonado *a* salmon-like
assar *vt* to roast; to grill; to bake; **~ no espeto** to barbecue; **~ no forno** to oven-bake
assaria *nf* grape variety
assazonado (sazonado) *a* seasoned; ripe
assedentado *a* thirsty
assentar *vt* to seat; to place; (of wine sediment &c) to settle; **~-se** *vi* to sit down
assento *nm* seat; chair; bench; *a* place to sit; (of bar) stool; (of wine) sediment
assidrar *vt* (of flavouring) to cider
assobiadeira *nf* pigeon
assustado *nm* [Braz] spur of the moment dance party
ástaco *nm* freshwater crayfish
astrágalo *nm* (of root beer flavouring) milk-vetch
atacado *nm* (of trading) wholesale
atapulhar *vt* to plug
atar *vt* (of poultry) to truss; to tie
até a vista! *excl* until next time! see you!
atenção *nf* courtesy; politeness
atencioso (atento) *a* courteous; polite
atestado *a* filled to the brim
atestar *vt* to fill to the brim; to cram
atesto *vt* (of wine evaporation) to top-up
atilamento *nm* punctuality
atmosfera *nf* atmosphere
atoalhado *nm* tablecloth, table-linen; *a* tablecloth-ed
atoalhar *nm* to cover with a tablecloth/table-linen
atoicinhado *a* larded
atomatar *vt* to mash; to squash
atonelado *a* (of barrel &c) tun-shaped
atóxico *a* (of mushroom &c) non-poisonous
atravessado *a* (of animal) cross-bred

atum *nm* tunny, tuna
auaduri *nm* [Braz] (of tree) lucuma (eggfruit)
auroque *nm* bison
auto (automóvel) *nm* car
autocarro *nm* bus
automóvel *nm* car; **~ de praça** taxi
avança *nm* [Braz] (of party) gate crasher
ave *nf* fowl; bird; **~s domésticas** poultry
aveia *nf* oats; oat; **sopa de ~** porridge; brose
avelã *nf* hazelnut
aveludado *a* (of wine) smooth; velvety
avena *nf* oats, oat
avental *nm* apron
aventar *vt* (of sugar-loaf) to separate from mould
avestruz *nm/f* ostrich
avicola *nm/f* poultry farmer
avicultura *nf* poultry farming
avila *nm* gourd/melon/cucumber fruit
avinagrar *vt* to vinegar
avinhado *a* wine-like
avinhar *vt* to (add/flavour with) wine
avitaminose *nf* vitamin deficiency
avitualhar *vt* to victual; to provision
aviú *nm* shrimp/prawn variety
azambujeiro (azambunjo) *nm* (of tree) wild olive
azebuado *a* [Braz] (of cattle) zebu, humped ox
azeda *nf* (of herb) wood sorrel
azedo(ê) *nm* sourness; sharpness; *a* sour; sharp; tart; off
azeitada *nf* glug of olive oil
azeitado *a* oily
Azeitão *nm* soft ewe's milk cheese
azeitar *vt* to (add) oil
azeite *nm* oil; olive oil; **~-de-cheiro** vegetable oil; palm oil; **~ de coco** palm oil; **~-de-dendê** palm oil; **~ doce** [Braz] olive oil; **~ virgem** virgin (olive) oil
azeiteira (azeiteiro *nm) nf* cruet
azeitinho *nm* [Braz] (of food additives) castor-oil
azeitona *nf* olive
azeitonar *vt* to add olives
azeitoneira *nf* olive plate
azeitoneiro *nm* olive-seller; olive plate
azereiro *nm* (of flavouring) Portuguese laurel cherry
azevia *nf* sea fish: sole
ázimo *a* unleavened; unfermented
azul *nm* blue
azuladinha *nf* [Braz] rum; hooch
azumbre *nm* liquid measure (approx 4 pints)

B

babá *nm* flour/eggs/milk cake;

[Braz] baby-sitter
bába-de-moça *nf* [Braz] cocoa-juice sweet
babador *nm* (of baby) bib; napkin
babar *vi* (of baby) to dribble
babugem *nf* (of food) left-overs
babugar *vt* (of food) to pick at
bacalhau *nm* sea fish: cod; (of dish) dried cod; **~ a bras** egg/potatoed cod; **~ curado** (of cod) dun-fish; **caras de ~** cod cheeks; **~ novo** codling; **~ seco (~ salgado)** dried cod, stockfish; **~ à Zé do Pipo** olived baked cod
bacalhoada *nf* cod dish
bacalhoeiro *nm* cod retailer; *a* cod-loving
bacanal *nf* bacchanalia; drunken revelry
bacelada *nf* newly-planted vineyard
bacelo *nm* newly-planted vine
bacia *nf* basin; wash-basin; washing-up bowl; frying-pan; baking-tin
baciada *nf* bowlful; basinful
bacífero *a* (of shrub &c) berry-bearing
bacon *nm* bacon
bácoro *nm* piglet; suck(l)ing pig
bacorote *nm* young pig
bacu *nm* [Braz] freshwater fish: catfish
bacucu *nm* Brazilian mollusc
bacu-pedra *nm* [Braz] freshwater fish: catfish
badana *nf* mutton of ewe
badejo *nm* sea fish: sea bass; grouper; whiting
badofe *nm* dish of ox lights; [Braz] shrimp/palm-oil dish
baé *nm* [Braz] pig variety
bafômetro *nm* breathalyser
baforada *nf* cigarette/cigar smoke
baforeira *nm* (of tree) caprifig; wild fig
baga *nf* berry; **~ de mirtilo** bilberry
bagaceira *nf* sugar-cane brandy; marc
bagaço *nm* crushed sugar-cane, bagasse; marc
bagagem *nf* luggage; **depósito de ~** cloakroom; left-luggage
bagalhão *nm* large berry
bagana *nf* cigarette/cigar end/butt
bago *nm* (of grape bunch) individual berry
bagoado *a* grape-like
bagre (mandi) (surubim-~) *nm* sea/freshwater fish: catfish
bagulhado (bagulhento) (bagulhoso) *a* seed-filled
bagulho *nm* grape-pip
baiacu *nm* [Braz] puffer fish; globefish
baila *nf* sea fish: spotted sea bass
bailar *vi* to dance

baile *nm* dance
baio *nm* maize cigarette
baionesa *nf* apple variety
bairari *nm* pigeon variety
baiúca *nf* down-market tavern; cheap-wine shop; pub; canteen
baiuqueiro *nm* inn-keeper; pub regular
baixar *vt* (of prices) to reduce; (of water temperature) to lower
baixela *nf* tableware; table setting
bala *nf* (of confectionery) sweet; candy [USA]; **~ de coco** coconut sweet; **~ de leite** toffee
balaieiro *nm* fruit/vegetable-seller
balança *nf* (of weight) scales
balançar *vt* to weigh
balata *nf* (of tree) bully tree, lucuma, chocky apple
balcão *nm* terrace; balcony; (of shop) counter; (of restaurant) bar
balchão *nm* Indian shrimp/oyster/pork/curry condiment
balde *nm* bucket; scuttle; dustbin; vat
baleia *nf* sea fish: whale
baleiro *nm* [Braz] street sweets-seller
balsa *nf* grape husk; mash-tub; cured-meat tub
balsâmico *a* balsamic
balsâmina-de-porga *nf* balsam apple
balseira *nf* [Braz] low quality sugar cane
balseiro *nm* mash-tub; mash-vat
bambá *nm* oil palm oil dregs
bambão *nm* jack tree fruit
bamboré *nm* (of plant Solanaceae) its fruit
bambu *nm* bamboo
bambueira *nf* bamboo shoot; bamboo plant
banana *nf* (of fruit) banana
banana-maçã *nf* [Braz] banana variety (small)
bananada *nf* (of confectionery) banana sweet
bananinha *nf* small banana; banana-shaped biscuit
bananose *nf* banana flour
banca *nf* table; [Braz] dinner-table
banco *nm* seat; bench; footstool; counter;
banda *nf* side
bandeja *nf* tray; board; salver; coaster
baneiro *nm* banana-seller
banha *nf* lard
banhar *vt* to wet
banheira *nf* bath
banheiro *nm* washroom; bathroom; bath; WC
banho *nm/f* bathing; bathe; bath; **~ de chuveiro** shower; **~-maria** double-saucepan, bain marie; **~ torco** turkish bath

banqueiro *nm* (of butcher) chopping block
banquete *nm* banquet; feast; dinner-party
banqueteador *nm* (of banquet) diner
banquetear *vi* to feast; to banquet
baobá *nm* (of tree) baobab; monkey-bread
baonesa (bionesa) *nf* eating apple variety
baquerubu *nm* (of plant) pea/ bean family
baquiqui *nm* (Braz] edible mollusc
baquité *nm* [Braz] basket
bar *nm* bar; bar counter; cafeteria; pub
barão *nm* (of beef) baron
baratíssimo *a* dirt-cheap
barato *a* cheap
baratômetro *nm* butter-making thermometer
barbado (piranambu) (barba-chata) (mandi-alumínio) *nm* [Braz] freshwater catfish
barbatana *nf* (of fish) fin
barbeiro *nm* surgeonfish
barbela *nf* (of cattle &c) dewlap
barbilhão (barbilho) (barbo) *nm* freshwater fish: barbel
barbudo *nm* [Braz] sea fish: barbudo, stout beardfish
bardana *nf* (of herb) burdock
barganhar *vi* to barter
barilha *nf* glasswort; marsh samphire
barquilho *nm* egg-filled boat-shaped pastry
barra *nf* (of soap) cake; (of chocolate/cereal) bar; **~ de touchino** bacon rasher
barracuda (bicuda) *nf* sea fish: barracuda
barrão *nm* boar
barrar *vt* (of butter/cream &c) to spread
barrasco *nm* young boar
barrenhão *nm* earthenware bowl
barrica *nf* keg; cask; barrel
barricão *nm* large barrel
barriga *nf* belly; **~ de perna** (of leg) calf
barrigada *nf* bellyful; sufficiency
barril *nm* barrel; **cerveja do ~** draft beer
barrilada *nf* barrel-ful
barrilete *nm* small barrel; firkin
barrilinho (barrilzinho) *nm* small barrel
barriqueiro *nm* cooper
barro *nm* clay; earthenware; earthenware pot/pan; pipkin
barrosã *a* (of cattle variety) barrosã
baselácea *nf* Ceylon spinach
bastardo *nm* sweet black grape variety
batadeira *nf* (of butter) churn
batedor *nm* beater; **~ de arame** wire beater/whisk; **~ de rodas** hand- whisk; **~ de varas** balloon whisk

batata *nf* potato; **~ assada** roast potato; **~ chips** potato chips; **~-doce** yam; sweet potato; **fécula de ~s** potato starch; **~s fritas** french fries, chips; fried potatoes; **~ frita rapidamente** sauté potatoes; **~-inglesa** baked potato; **~ a murro** baked potato; **purê de ~s** mashed potatoes

batatada *nf* potatoes in quantity; (of confectionery) potato sweet

batatarana *nf* (of vine) seaside bean

batateiro *a* potato-fancying

batatinha *nf* small potato; white potato; **~s fritas** chips; crisps

bate-bate *nm* (of drink) sugar-cane brandy-sour

batedeira *nf* (of butter) churn; **~ de ovos** egg whisk; beater

batedor de ovos *nm* egg whisk

bater *vt* to beat; to stir; to mix; to shake

bateria *nf* (of utensils) kitchen set

batida *nf* [Braz] brandy sour; egg-nogg; cachaça or vodka fruit/sugar/ice cocktail

batido *nm* heavily-shaken drink; **~ de leite** milk-shake

batismo *nm* (of milk/wine &c) dilution

batizamento *nm* christening feast

batoca *nf* variety of grape

batuera (batueira) *nf* corn-cob

baunilha *nf* vanilla

bauru *nm* toasted ham/cheese/ tomato-sandwich

bazófia *nf* left-overs stew

bazulaque *nm* liver stew; [Braz] (of confectionery) coconut/honey sweet; badly-cooked food

beatinha *nf* sea fish: scorpion fish

bêbado *a* tipsy

bebedouro *nm* drinking fountain; well

beber *vt* to drink; to swallow; to sip; to absorb

bêbera *nf* early-ripening fig

beberar *vi* to quench one's thirst

beberes *nm* drinks; spirits

beberete *nm* aperitif; cocktail; drinks party; cocktail party

bebericação *nf* drinking; sip

bebericador *nm* tippler; *a* tippling

bebericar *vt* to drink; to sip at

beberrão (beberraz) (beberrote) *nm* drunkard

bebes (beberes) *nm* drinks

bebida *nf* drink; cup; **~s alcoólicas** spirits; alcoholic drinks; **~ fermentada (~ fervida)** brew; **~ gelada** (of drink) frappé

bebido *a* (of thirst) quenched; (of condition) drunk

bebível *a* (of water &c quality) drinkable

bechamel *nm* (of sauce) béchamel
beguaba (beguava) *nm* clam variety
beiço *nm* rim; lip
beijar *vt* (of bottle) to open; to crack
beijinho *nm* (of confectionery) coconut sweet
beijo-de-moça *nm* (of confectionery) sugar/egg sweet
beijo-frio *nm* chocolate-covered ice-cream
beiju (beijuaçu) *nm* tapioca-cake
beijupirá *nm* [Braz] sergeant fish
beilhó *nm/f* pumpkin-filled wafer
beirute *nm* pitta sandwich with filling of choice
beluca *nf* (of fish) beluga
bem *adv* (eg of seasoning) well; **~ passado** (of steak) well done; **passe ~!** goodbye!
bem-casado *nm* biscuit variety
bem-vindo *a* welcome
bênção da mesa *nf* (before meals) grace
benjoeiro *nm* (of seasoning berry) spicebush
benzina *nf* petrol; gasoline
berbigão *nm* cockle
bergamota *nf* bergamot; [Braz] (of orange) mandarin; tangerine
berinjela *nf* egg-plant, aubergine
berjaçote *nm* fig variety
bernaca *nf* brent-goose
bernarda *nf* pear variety
besugo *nm* sea fish: sea bream
betara (embetara) (papa-terra) *nf* sea fish: southern kingfish
beterraba (betarraba) *nf* beetroot; sugar-beet
bezerro *nm* (bull) calf
biaribu *nm* [Braz] hot-earth-pit cooking
bica *nf* bread variety; sea fish: sea bream; blended cow/goat/ewe's milk semi-soft cheese; (of coffee) espresso
bicada *nf* [Braz] sip of brandy
bicado *a* [Braz] tipsy
bicarbonato de sódio *nm* bicarbonate of soda; baking powder
bicho de cozinha *nm* kitchen hand; scullion
bico *nm* (of fowl) beak; poultry; (of coffee-pot) spout; (of gas) burner; **~s** piping-bag
bico-de-pato (jurupensém) *nm* [Braz] freshwater fish: duck-bill
bico-rasteiro *nm* american snipe
bicuda (barracuda) *nf* sea fish: guaguanche; barracuda
bidêt *nm* bidet
bidó *nm* cassava (manioc) cake
bifada *nf* beefsteak

bife *nm* (of beef) steak; **~ a cavalo** steak with fried egg; **~ de filé mignon** sirloin steak; **~ grelhado** grilled steak; **~ (muito) mal passado** (very) underdone (rare) steak; **~ a pé** (of dish) steak/eggs/potatoes; **~ ao ponto** medium-cooked steak; **~ a portuguesa** (of dish) port wine-sauced grilled/sautéed steak; fried-egged minute steak; **~ rolê** beef-roll

bifesteque *nm* (of beef) steak

bigarrade *nm* (of bitter orange sauce) bigarade

biju ([Braz] **beiju**) *nm* cassava (manioc) cake

bijungarias *nf* [Braz] delicacy; dish; food

bijupirá *nm* [Braz] sea fish: cobia, runner, sergeant fish

bilha *nf* pitcher; earthenware bottle

bilhete *nm* ticket

binga *nf* cigarette lighter

biodegradável *a* biodegradable

biongo *nm* tavern

biqueira *nf* [Braz] cigarette-holder

biqueirão *nm* sea fish: anchovy

biribá *nm* biriba fruit

biribarana *nf* [Braz] (of tree) custard apple variety

birita *nf* [Braz] (any) alcoholic drink; **tomar uma ~** to have a drink *(usu* white rum)

biró *nm* bit, piece, morsel

biroró *nm* [Braz] cassava (manioc) cake

bis *adv* (of entertainment) encore!

bisão *nm* bison

biscoiteira (biscouteira) *nf* biscuit tray; biscuit plate

biscoiteiro *nm* biscuit seller; biscuit maker

biscoito (biscouto) *nm* biscuit; shortcake; tea-cake; rusk; cracker; scone; bun; **~ amanteigado seco** shortbread; **~ amanteigados** butter-biscuits; **~ fino** cracker; **~ em forma de colher** sponge-finger

bispo *nm* burnt-flavour

bisteca de boi *nf* T-bone steak

bistrô *nm* bistro

bivalve *a* (of mullusc) bivalve

blender (liquidificador) *nm* blender

blênio *nm* sea fish: blenny

boa-tarde! *excl* good afternoon!

boal *nm* (of wine) medium-sweet madeira

bobéia *nf* (of bread) crumb

bobó *nm* [Braz] shrimp/cassava/bean/banana/coconut-oil dish

bobulha *nf* (of plant) shoot

boca *nf* mouth; throat, gullet; (of barrel) tap-hole; bung

boca-de-fogo *nm* sea fish: snapper variety

boca-lisa *nf* [Braz] freshwater fish: catfish
bocada *nf* mouthful; bite; gulp
bocado *nm* mouthful; bit
bocal *nm* (of bottle &c) mouth; (of candlestick) candle-holder
bochecho *nm* mouthful; small quantity of liquid
boda *nf* wedding feast; **~s de diamante** diamond wedding; **~s de ouro** golden wedding; **~s de prata** silver wedding
bodalha *nf* young pig
bode *nm* billy-goat
bodega *nf* wine cellar
bodegueiro (bodegão) *nm* wine-cellar owner; inn-keeper
bodiano (bodião) *nm* sea fish: wrasse
boga (boga-do-mar) *nf* sea fish: sea bream
boi *nm* bull; bullock; ox; bovine animal; **~-com-folhagens** [Braz] (of beef) steak/lettuce salad
boi-vivo *nm* [Braz] ox-testicle stew
bóia *nf* [Braz] meal; food; provisions
boião *nm* jar; pot
boiar *vt* [Braz] to eat; to dine
bojarda *nf* pear variety
bojo *nm* (of bottle &c) belly
bola *nf* (of meat &c) ball
bolacha *nf* biscuit; cracker; wafer; **~ de gengibre** ginger-snap; **~ torrada** crisp biscuit
bolacheiro *nm* biscuit-seller/ maker
bolachinha *nf* small biscuit
boleima *nf* plain cake
boleto *nm* (of mushroom) boletus
bolhelho *nm* cake
bolinho *nm* biscuit; wafer; waffle; small cake; dumpling; (of meat &c) ball; faggot; **~s de fubá** fried maize bread
bolo *nm* cake; bun; dumpling; **~ branco com baunilha** angel-cake; **~ de casamento** wedding-cake; **~ de cenoura** carrot cake; **~ de claras** angel-cake; **~ de creme** cream-cake; **~ de fubá** cornmeal cake; **~ de gengibre** gingerbread; **~ inglés** English cake; **~ de peixe** fish-cake; **~ de queijo** cheesecake; **~ de sorvete** ice-cream tart
bolo-podre *nm* [Braz] raised cake
bolonhesa (à) *a* meat-sauced
bolor *nm* (of decay) mould
bom *a* good; large; **~-bocado** *nm* (of confectionery) peanut/ coconut/sugar sweet; **~-dia!** good morning!!; **boa-noite!** goodnight!; **boa-tarde!** good afternoon
bomba *nf* (of pastry) éclair; (of chocolate/cream) puff; (of ice-cream) bombe; **~ de chope** beer-pump
bombilha *nf* maté straw

bombom *nm* (of confectionery) sweet; bonbon; chocolates; **~ de licor** chocolate liqueur

bona-xira *nf* sumptuous meal; rich groaning table

boneca *nf* bouquet garni

bonita *nf* cassava (manioc) pastry

bonito (serra-comum) (sarda) *nm* sea fish: bonito; skipjack tuna

boquilha (piteira) *nf* cigar/ cigarette-holder

Borba *nm* Alentejo vineyard

borbotão *nm* (of boiling water) bubbling-up

borbotar *vt* to boil; to bubble

borbulhante *nf* [Braz] sugar-cane brandy; *a* bubbling

borda *nf* brim; rim

bordadura *nf* (of decoration) trimming

bordalo *nm* freshwater fish: carp variety; minnow

bordo *nm* (of tree) maple

Borgonha *nf* (of wine) Burgundy

bororó *nm* pampean deer

borra *nf* sediment, lees, grounds, dregs

borracho *nm* young pigeon; *a* tipsy

borragem *nf* (of herb) borage

borrega *nf* (of sheep) ewe lamb; sucking ewe

borrego *nm* (of sheep) lamb; sucking lamb

borrelho (burrié) *nm* winkle, periwinkle

borro *nm* 1-2 year-old ram

bota *nf* barrel; wine cask; leather bottle; tub

botão *nm* bud

botão-de-farda *nm* amaranth; popcorn grain

botelha *nf* bottle; bottle-of-wine

botelharia *nf* wine-cellar

botelheiro *nm* butler

botequim *nm* tavern, pub, bar; coffee-house/bar

botequineiro *nm* inn-keeper; bar-keeper; coffee-house owner

botija *nf* jar; stone jug

botoado *nm* catfish variety

bovino *nm* bullock; *a* bovine

braço *nm* (of pork &c) hand; **~-de-moça (jerepoca) (jurupoca) (liro)** freshwater catfish

branca *nf* rum

brancagem *nf* bread/meat tax

branco *a* white; **manjar ~** blancmange; **molho ~** white sauce; **pão ~** white bread; *nm* white wine

brando *a* tender

branquear *vt* to blanch

braseiro (braseira *nf) nm* warming dish; chafing dish; small stove

brasido *nm* hot coals; embers

Brasil *nm* Brazil

brasileiras *nfpl* (of confectionery) sweets

brasílio *a* Brazilian
brema *nf* freshwater fish: bream
breve *a* short; quick; **até ~!** see you soon!
brigadeiro *nm* (of confectionery) butter/milk/ chocolate sweet
brindar *vt* to drink the health of; to toast
brinde *nm* (of salutation) toast
brioche *nf* brioche
briol *nm* wine
briquete *nm* (of charcoal &c) briquette
britadas *nfpl* crushed olives
broa *nf* unleavened maize/rice bread/cake, pone
brocar *vt* (of vegetables &c) to scoop out
brocojó *nm* [Braz] cake variety
brócolis *nmpl* broccoli; calabrese
broeiro *nm* maize-bread seller
bromeliácea *nf* (of plant) pineapple
brota *nf* spring; fountain
brote *nm* [Braz] biscuit
brulho *nm* olive husks
bruto *a* (of wine) brut
Bucelas *nm* wine-growing region
bucha *nf* mouthful; bite; chunk of bread; dishcloth gourd
bucho *nm* tripe; pork sausage; (of bird) craw, crop
bufa-de-lobo *nf* (of mushroom) puffball
búfalo *nm* buffalo, bison
bufete *nm* buffet; side-board; dresser; cupboard; bar
bugia *nf* candle-stick
bule *nm* teapot
buquê *nm* (of flowers) bouquet; bunch of flowers
burbom *nm* [Braz] (of shrub) coffee variety
buré *nm* Indian corn porridge
bureva *nf* [Braz] freshwater fish: variety of catfish
burneira *a* (of grapes) juicy
burro *nm* donkey
buruso *nm* fruit-residue; grape-skins
butano *nm* (of gas) butane
butargas *nf* [Braz] pickled fish-eggs
butelo *nm* hog's tail sausage
butirada *nf* butter cake
búxulo *nm* bearberry
búzio *nm* whelk; conch

C

caá *nm* [Braz] maté
caacuí *nf* [Braz] new leaf of the maté plant
caarina *nm* [Braz] cassava root, manioc
cabaça *nf* bottle gourd
cabaçada *nf* gourdful
cabaceiro (~-amargoso) [Braz]) *nm* bottle gourd
cabacinha *nf* small gourd; egg gourd; orange gourd
cabaço *nm* calabash; bottle

gourd; sea fish: swallow fish; sapphirine gurnard
cabaneiro *(cabano)* *nm* large wicker basket
cabaré *nm* cabaret
cabeça *nf* head; **~-azul** (of fish) dorado; **~-de-urubu** [Braz] chocolate tree
cabelo *nm* hair; **~-de-anjo** [Braz] vermicelli
cabide *nm* clothes-rack/stand; hat rack/stand; clothes hanger
cabidela *nf* giblets, stewed giblets
cabina telefônica *nf* telephone box
cabiú *nm* [Braz] juice of manioc tubers
cabo *nm* handle
caboz *nm* sea fish: goby
cabra *nf* nanny-goat; sea fish: red mullet; goatfish; gurnard; **~ morena** grey gurnard; **~ transmontano** semi-hard goat cheese; **~ vermelha** red gurnard
cabrão *nm* billy-goat; **~ montês** (of goat) ibex
cabreiro *nm* goat's milk cheese
cabrinha *nf* (of goat) kid; sea fish: gurnard; [Braz] mango
cabrito (~a) *nm(f)* (of goat) kid
cabriúva *nf* brandied omelette; brandy/sugar/ginger drink
cabronaz *nm* large billy-goat
cabucho *nm* sugar-loaf coned end
cabuçu *nm* [Braz] armadillo
caça *nf* (of hunting) game; **~ de penas** game-birds
caçada *nf* hunt; shoot
cação *nm* sea fish; skate; shark; [Braz] cassava (manioc) soup/drink; **~-anjo** sea fish: angel-fish; skate; **~-da-areia** sea fish: sand shark; **~-de-espinho** *nm* sea fish: spiny dogfish; **~-garoupa** [Braz] sea fish: grouper-shark; **~-martelo** sea fish: hammerhead-shark; **~-prego** sea fish: spiny dogfish
caçaroba *nf* [Braz] pigeon
caçarola *nf* saucepan; (of pan) casserole
cacau *nm* cocoa; cacau; **gordura de ~** cocoa-butter
cacau-do-peru *nm* (of cacao) patashte
cacaurana *nf* (of tree) chocolate tree
caçava (caçave) *nf* cassava (manioc) flour
caceta *nf* colander; strainer; sieve; [Port] soup ladle; tablespoon
cacha *nf* (of orange &c) half
cachaça (pinga) *nf* (of alcohol) white rum; sugar-cane spirits
cachaço *nm* neck; [Braz] breeding-boar
cachão *nm* vigourous boiling
cachara (pintado) (surubim) *nm* freshwater fish: stripped catfish
cacheado *a* [Braz] (of fruit

types) clustered, bunched
cachimbada *nf* (of pipe) tobacco smoke; (of tobacco) pipeful
cachimbador *nm* pipe-smoker
cachimbar *vi* to smoke a pipe
cachimbo *nm* (of smoking) pipe
cacho *nm* (of grapes &c) bunch; cluster
cacholeira *nf* pork liver sausage
cachorra *nf* (of animal) bitch; sea fish: albacore; long-fin tunny; freshwater fish: paraya
cachorro *nm* [Braz] sea fish: fiddler-fish; **~-quente** hot-dog
cachudo *nm* grape variety; *a* (of grapes &c) large-clustered
cacica *nf* [Braz] palm-oil/pepper/pumpkin-pips/chicken casserole
caço *nm* saucepan; casserole; ladle; large spoon; earthenware frying-pan
caçoila *nf* casserole; earthenware cooking pot
caçoleta *nf* small frying-pan
cacongo *nm* African salmon
caçoula *nf* casserole; earthenware cooking pot
cacto *nm* cactus
caçuiroba *nf* pigeon variety
cadeira *nf* seat; chair; place; **~ de bar** bar-stool; **~ de braços** arm-chair; easy-chair; **~ de criança** baby chair; **~ de preguiça** deck-chair; **~ de rodas** wheelchair
cadelinha *nf* (of clam) wedge shell
cadivo *a* over-ripe
cadorna *nf* quail
café *nm* coffee; café; bar [USA] **borra de ~** coffee grounds; **~-caneca** [Braz] lowly bar; **~-concerto** music/coffee-house; **~ dançante** coffee-house with dancing; **~ descafeinado** decaffeinated coffee; **~ expresso** espresso coffee; **~ fraco** weak coffee; **grão de ~** coffee-bean; **~ à inglesa** coffee with a splash of milk; **~-com-isca** [Braz] lightly brandied coffee; coffee with titbits; **jogo (serviço) de ~** coffee set; **~ com leite** white coffee, café au lait; café latte; **~ sem leite** black coffee; **~ de manhã** breakfast coffee; **~-com-mistura** coffee with delicatessen; **moinho de ~** coffee-mill; **~ com preto** black coffee; **sucedâneo do ~** ersatz coffee; coffee substitute; **~ torrado** roasted coffee
cafedório *nm* weak coffee
cafeína *nf* caffeine
cafelista *nm/f* coffee planter; coffee owner; [Braz] coffee addict
cafeteira *nf* coffee-pot; percolator; **~ com torneira** coffee urn

cafeteiro *nm* coffee-house owner; barman
cafezeiro *nm* coffee
cafezinho *nm* small cup of coffee *(usu* black); **hora de ~** coffee-break
cafezista *nm/f* coffee planter; coffee-lover
cafofa *nf* [Braz] cassava-ed roasted jerked beef
cafumango *nm* ship's cook
cagaiteira *nf* [Braz] (of tree) myrtle
caiabana *nf* cassava variety
caiana *nf* [Braz] rum; sugar-cane variety
caicau *nm* black fig
caiçuma *nf* thickened cassava (manioc) juice dish
caieira *nf* bonfire
caiena *nf* banana variety; **pimenta-de-~** cayenne pepper
caimito *nm* [Braz] star apple
caipirinha *nf* [Braz] iced white rum/lemon drink
cairi *nm* [Braz] spicy chicken stew
caixa *nf* box; container; vessel; receptacle; bin; **~ de cerveja** crate (case) of beer; **de papelão** carton; **~ registradora** cash-register
caixote do lixo *nm* dustbin
cajá (~-mirim) *nm* hog-plum; **~-manja** [Braz] (of fruit) otaheite apple
caju *nm* cashew-nut
cajuada *nf* [Braz] cashew-nut juice drink; (of confectionery) cashew-nut sweet
cajuína *nf* cashew wine
cajuzinho *nm* (of confectionery) cashew-shaped peanut sweet
cala *nf* (of fruit &c) cut-out sample
calabrear *vt* (of wine &c) to adulterate; to season
calafate *nm* barberry
calamar *nm* squid; cuttlefish
calaminta *nf* calamint
cálamo *nm* stalk
calandra *nf* lark
calapídeos *nm* gladiator box crab
calar *vt* (of fruit &c testing) to plug
calda *nf* syrup; preserved fruit
caldear *vt* to eat soup
caldeira *nf* kettle; **~ de pressão** pressure-cooker; **~ a vapor** steaming pan
caldeirão *nm* large pan
caldeirada *nf* kettle-ful; fish-stew, chowder
caldeireta *nf* mug; tankard
caldeiro *nm* casserole; cooking-pot; cooker
caldo *nm* sauce; soup, broth; hotch-potch; **~ de cana** sugar-cane juice; **~ de carne** consommé, beef-tea; beef stock (of cubes) stock cubes; **~ de peixe** fish soup; fish stock; **~ verde** potato/

cabbage soup
caldo-de-feijão *nm* dove variety
caldoso *a* succulent; juicy; soupy
calefator *nm* heater; radiator
cálice *nm* wine/liqueur-glass
cálido *a* hot; heated
caloria *nf* calorie; **sem ~** calorie-free
calorífico *a* (of value) calorific
calumbá *nf* [Braz] sugar-cane juice
cama *nf* bed; sofa; **~ de casal** double-bed; **~ e mesa** board and lodging
camada *nf* layer; covering
camafeu *nm* (of confectionery) sugared nut sweet
camapu *nm* cape gooseberry; ground-cherry, strawberry-tomato
câmara *nf* room, bedroom; **~ frigorífica** cold-store
camará-branco *nm* [Braz] yerba (maté) sagrada
camarão *nm*; prawn; shrimp; **~-de-água-doce** freshwater crayfish; **~ões marinados** potted shrimps; **~-rosa** pink prawn; pink shrimp; **~ tigre** tiger prawn
camaratinga *nf* (of herbal tea) yerba (maté) sagrada
camargo *nm* [Braz] sweet white coffee
camarinha *nf* room; bedroom; (of plant) crowberry;
cambará-branco *nm* (of herbal tea) yerba (maté) sagrada
cambeva *nm* hammerhead shark
cambica *nf* [Braz] (of dish) cassava-ed cherries
câmbio *nm* (of money) change
cambito *nm* leg of pork; (of cloakroom) hat-stand; coat-hanger
camboatá *nm* catfish
cambucá (cambuci) *nm* (of fruit) myrtle
cambuí *nm* (of fruit) myrtle
cambulha (cambulhada) *nf* bunch of keys
cambuquira *nf* [Braz] (of dish) pumpkin vine-shoots/roast beef
câmera *nf* camera
camoesa *nf* (of apple) pippin
campainha *nf* small bell
campestre *a* field; wild
campina *nf* free-range chicken
campino *nm* farmer; countryman
campo *nm* (of countryside) field
camurça *nf* chamois; mountain goat
camurupim (tarpão) (pirapema) (pema) *nm* sea fish: tarpon; silverfish
cana (~-de-açúcar) *nf* sugar-cane
cana-do-brejo *nf* (of spice) cardamom
canapé *nm* canapé, nibble; (of

seating) sofa
canapu *nm* ground cherry
canarana *nf* millet
canastrada *nf* basketful
canastrel *nm* basket; hamper
cancha *nf* abattoir
cande *a* (of fruit) crystallized
candeeiro *nm* chandelier; candelabrum
candeia *nf* light; lamp; candle
candela *nf* light; lamp
candelabro *nm* chandelier; candelabrum
candelinha *nf* small candle
candial *a* (of wheat) very white
cândida *nf* white rum; sugar-cane brandy
candil *nm* light; lamp; candle; *a* (of fruit) crystallized
candilar *vt* (of fruit) to crystallize
candiru-branco *nm* [Braz] Amazon freshwater fish: whale catfish
caneca *nf* mug; tankard; cup
caneco *nm* (of mug) stein; deep mug
caneja *nf* sea fish: dogfish
canela *nf* (of spice) cinnamon; (of meat) shin
canelão *nm* (of confectionery) sugared cinnamon sweet
canelar *vt* (of meat &c) to make an incision
caneleira (caneleiro *nm) nf* cinnamon
canequinha *nf* cream-jug
cangaço *nm* pressed-fruit skin
cangati *nm* freshwater fish: catfish
canguara *nf* white rum; sugar-cane brandy
cangulo *nm* sea fish: triggerfish
cangurro *nm* sea fish: triggerfish
canguru *nm* kangaroo
cangurupi *nm* sea fish: tarpon
canha *nf* white rum; sugar-cane brandy
canhanha *nf* sea fish: sea bream
caninha *nf* white rum; sugar-cane brandy
canivete *nm* knife
canja *nf* rice/pasta/vegetables chicken-soup; **~ alho-porro** cock-a-leekie
canjica *nf* milk/maize/cinnamon sweet soup; coconut/cinnamon/corn dish
canjirão *nm* wide-mouthed wine-jug
cannelloni *nmpl* cannelloni
cantã *nf* arrowroot variety
cantaleira *nf* dish-rack
cantalupo *nm* cantaloup melon
cantarilho do norte *nm* sea fish: redfish
cântaro *nm* jar; jug; earthenware pot; can
cantina *nf* canteen; inn; (of armed forces) mess
cantineiro (~a) *nm(f)* inn-keeper
cantinho *nm* (of bread) slice
canudinho *nm* (of drinking)

straw; (of cream) horn
canudo de chupar *nm* (of drinking) straw
cão *nm* dog
capa *nf* cover; covering
capacho *nm* mat
capacidade *nf* capacity
capadete *nm* [Braz] castrated piglet
capado *nm* castrated-ram, -goat, -boar
capão *nm* capon
caparari *nm* stripped catfish
capela *nf* garland; **~-de-cheiros** bouquet garni; herbed sauce
capelim *nm* sea fish: capelin
caperotada *nf* minced chicken (&c) stew
capetão *nm* bean/flour baguette
capilé *nm* capillaire, maidenhair-fern orange-flower water syrup
capim-cidreira (**~-de-cheiro** [Braz]) *nm* lemon grass
capim-depnossa-senhora *nm* (of cereal) Job's tears
capitão-chico *nm* crossbreed of Brazilian swine
capitoso *a* (of wine) heady
capoeiro *nm* [Braz] small deer variety
caporal *nm* coarse tobacco
cappuccino *nm* cappuccino
capro *nm* billy-goat
cápsula *nm* (of seed) pod; husk
caqui *nm* [Braz] kaki; japanese persimmon fruit
caquizeiro *nm* kaki; japanese persimmon fruit
cará *nm* [Braz] variety of yam; freshwater fish: southern kingfish
carabiniero *nm* red prawn
caracol (**caracóis** *pl) nm* (of mollusc) snail; (of plant) snail-flower (snap beans)
cara-fechada *nm* [Braz] sugar-loaf
cará-inhame *nm* white yam
cará-mimosa *nf* cush-cush; tropical yam
cara-quebrada *nf* broken sugar-loaf
caracoleta *nf* snail
caracu *nm* [Braz] cattle variety
carajé *nm* [Braz] (of cake) icing
carambola *nf* (of fruit) kiwi, Chinese gooseberry
caramburu *nm* Indian corn drink
caramelado *nm* caramel sweet
caramelizar *vi* to caramelize
caramelo *nm* caramel
caramujo *nm* cabbage variety; periwinkle
carandá-guaçu *nm* muriti palm, brazilian wine palm
caranguejo *nm* crab; **carne de ~** dressed crab
caranha *nf* [Braz] freshwater fish: black pacu; **~-do-mangue** [Braz] sea fish: grey snapper
caranho *nm* [Braz] sea fish: lutjanid; **~-vermelho** *nm* sea

fish: mutton-snapper, mutton-fish
carapau (xarelete) (xerelete) *nm* sea fish: mackerel shad; blue runner
carapeba-listada *nf* [Braz] sea fish: patao
carapela *nf* Indian-corn husk
carapinhada *nf* frozen drink (*esp* lemonade/orangeade)
carapinheira *nf* (of tree) pear variety
carapitanga *nf* sea fish: bastard-snapper
carapó *nm* [Braz] sea fish: carapo, electric eel
carássio *nm* freshwater fish: crucian carp
carataí *nm* [Braz] freshwater fish: catfish
caratinga *nf* sea fish: mojarra
caratuã *nf* roasted dried game
caravela *nf* cassava (manioc) stalk
caraxué-da-capoeira *nf* (of bird) thrush
carboidrato *nm* carbohydrate
carça *nf* barnacle
carcaça *nf* carcass
carcharídeos *nmpl* sand-shark
carcinicultura *nf* crustacean-rearing
cardamomo *nm* (of spice) cardamom
cardápio *nm* menu; **~ do dia** set menu
cardigueira *nf* [Braz] wild dove variety
cardiídeos *nmpl* cockle
cardo-silvestre *nm* prickly artichoke
careteira *nf* balsam apple
carga *nf* (of merchandise) goods
cargo *nm* bread
cariacu *nm* fallow deer
caribé *nm* cassava (manioc) drink; cassava (manioc) porridge; avocado delicacy
caribu *nm* caribou
caridade *nf* (of tea-party) cake
caril *nm* curry; curry-sauce
carimã *nf* [Braz] cassava (manioc) cake; cassava (manioc) flour
carioca *a* (of hot drink) coffee
cariz *nm* caraway; caraway seed
carnadura *nf* meat quality
carnaval *nm* carnival
carne *nf* meat; flesh; **~-a-~** pressed salted anchovies; **~ bovina** beef; **~-de-ceará (~-seca) (~-do-sertão) (~-do-sul) (~-de-sol) (jabá)** sun-dried meat; salted meat; **~ enlatada (~ salgada)** bully/corned-(beef); **~ maturada** aged beef; **~ moída** minced beef; **~ do peito** brisket; **~-de-vento** *nf* jerked meat
carnear *vt* (of cattle) to slaughter
carneiro (~a) *nm(f)* sheep, (ewe); lamb; mutton
carniça *nf* meat; offal

carniçaria *nf* butcher's
carniceiro *nm* butcher
carnoso *a* meaty
carocho *nm* sea fish: kitefin shark; portuguese dogfish
caroço *nm* (of fruit) stone; pip; (of apple) core
caroçudo *a* (of fruit) stone-containing; pip-containing
carolina *nf* light bun
carolo *nm* (of pineapple &c) fibrous core; **~s de milho** coarse-crushed maize
carpa *nf* freshwater fish: carp
carpaccio *nm* carpaccio; thinly sliced raw beef/tuna/veal/fish
carrapicho-grande *nm* burdock
carrascão *nm* brandy-added wine
carrega-bestas *nf* grape variety
carretilha *nf* pastry-cutting wheel
carrinho *nm* trolley; **~ de chá** tea-trolley
carro *nm* car; **~ de praça** taxi
carta *nf* menu
cartão de crédito *nm* credit card; **~ de visita** business card; visiting card
carteira *nf* (of money) wallet
cartilagem *nf* gristle
caruera *nf* [Braz] clumps of grated manioc (cassava)
carumbá *nm* bucket
caruncho *nm* breed of Brazilian swine
caruru *nm* [Braz] prawn/okra/chili/dendê-oil dish
caruru-azedo *nm* [Braz] roselle, Jamaica sorrel
carvão *nm* charcoal
carvoaria *nm* charcoal shop
casa comum *nf* WC
casa *nf* house; **feito em ~** home-made
casaca *nf* evening dress
casadinhos *nm* jam biscuits
casal *nm* farm; (of game birds) brace
casca *nf* skin; peel; husk; rind; bark; **~ de caneleira** cinnamon; **com ~** (of potatoes) jacket
casca-preciosa *nf* sassafras
cascabulho *nm* (of chestnuts &c) skin
cascão *nm* shell; peel
cascar *vt* to peel; to shell
cascarrão *nm* skin; shell; hull
casco *nm* keg; cask; barrel; [Braz] empty bottle; **~ velho** carcass
cascudo *nm* [Braz] freshwater catfish
caseação *nf* cheese-making
caseificar *vt* to cheese-make
caseiforme *a* cheesey
caseiro *a* home-made; home-cooked
caseoso (queijoso) *a* cheesy
cassaco *nm* opossum variety
cássia *nf* cassia
cassino *nm* casino
castanha *nf* chestnut; **~-d'água**

water-chesnut; **~-do-pará** Brazil nut
castanhola *nf* sea fish: snapper
castelo *nm* whipped stiff egg white; **~ branco** soft ewe or goat cheese
castiçal *nm* candle-stick
casulo *nm* pod
cata *nf* [Braz] (of roasted coffee) bean-grading
catador *nm* [Braz] coffee grading machine
catapereiro *nm* wild pear tree
cataplana *nf* cooking-pot; steamer; (of dish) mussels/ sausage/bacon/herbs; seafood stew; meat stew; fish stew
catauari *nm* [Braz] (of shrub) caper variety
categorizar *vt* to grade
catimplora *nf* wine/water cooler; ice-cream freezer
catimpuera *nf* fermented cassava (manioc) honey drink
catupiri *nm* cream cheese
catuta [Braz] *nf* sugar-cane brandy
cauaba *nf* [Braz] drinking vessel
cauim *nm* [Braz] fermented cassava (manioc) fruit drink
caule *nm* stalk; stem
caulim (caulino) *nm* (of clay) kaolin; china clay
cava *nf* cellar
cavaca *nf* biscuit; cake
cavala *nf* sea fish: mackerel; spanish mackerel; **~-wahoo (wahoo)** sea fish: wahoo
cavalão *nm* horse; sea fish: mackerel
cavalinha *nf* sea fish: small mackerel
cavalo *nm* horse; **~ pequeno** bidet
cavanejo *nm* wicker basket
cavaqueira *nf* biscuit-seller
caviar *nm* caviar; **~ vermelho** red caviar
caxiri (caxirim) *nm* (of confectionery) cassava sweet; casiri beer
caxixe *nm* [Braz] chayote, cucumber-like fruit, choko, chocho
caxixi *nf* poor quality white rum
cear *vi* to take supper
ceará *nf* [Braz] jerked beef
ceata *nf* feast; banquet
cebola *nf* onion; **~-branca** shallot; **rodelas de ~** onion rings
cebola-de-cheiro *nf* Welsh onion
cebolada *nf* onion stew; onion dish
cebolinha-capim (cebolinho *nm) nf* chive
cedinho *adv* (of morning) very early
cedo *adv* early
cega-rega *nf* cicada, cricket
ceguinho *nm* [Braz] freshwater fish: catfish
cela *nf* (of honeycomb) cell

celeireiro *nm* cellarman
celeiro *nm* cellar
celga *nf* beet
celha *nm* fish-basket; kit
cem *nm* one hundred
cenáculo *nm* dining-room; (of monastery &c) refectory; (of army) mess-room
cenário (cenatório *nm) a* supper
cenoura *nf* carrot
centafolho *nm* tripe
centeio *nm* rye
centígrado *a* centigrade
centilitro *nm* centilitre
cepa *nf* onion; vine
cepo *nm* butcher's block
cera *nf* wax; candle; **~ de abelha** beeswax
cerâmica *nf* ceramics; earthenware
céramo *nm* clay vase
cerasina *nf* cherry drink
cereal (cereais *pl) nm* cereal; corn; breadstuff
cerefólio (cerefolho) *nm* chervil
cereja *nf* cherry; **licor de ~s** cherry-brandy
cerejeira *nf* (of tree) cherry; **~-das-antilhas (~-do-pará)** Barbados cherry
cernambi *nm* [Braz] mollusc: clam variety
cerro *nm* (of cup &c) residual liquid
cervato *nm* young deer
cervo (~a) *nm(f)* deer (doe)
cerveja *nf* beer; ale; **~ amarga (~ de barril)** bitter; **~ clara** light beer; lager; **~ escura e forte** stout; **~ forte** export ale; **~ fresca do barril** draught; **~ grande** large beer; **~ inglesa** bitter; **~ leve** lager; **~ pequena** small beer; **~ preta** dark beer
cervejada *nf* glass of beer; group of beer-drinkers; **~s-de-barbante** [Braz] root-beer
cervejar *vi* to drink beer
cervejaria *nf* pub; brewery
cervejeiro *nm* brewer
cervo *nm* deer
cesta *nf* basket
cestada *nf* basketful
cestão *nm* large basket
cesto *nm* (of bread) basket; hamper
cetáceo *nm* whale
céu da boca *nm* (of mouth) palate; roof of mouth
cevada *nf* barley; **~ cevadinha** pearl-barley; **farinha de ~** barley-meal
cevador *nm* [Braz] maté host
cevão *nm* fattened hog
cevar *vt* (of pig &c) to fatten; to place maté in cup; to prepare cassava flour; to entertain lavishly
chá *nm* tea; tea-party; **aparelho de ~** tea service; **bandeja de ~** tea-tray; **~ de camomila** camomile tea; **carrinho para servir ~** tea-

trolley; ~ **das cinco horas** afternoon tea; **colher de ~** teaspoon; ~ **com limão** lemon tea; **~-de-cozinha** bridal hen tea-party; ~ **dançante** tea-dancing; ~ **gelado** iced tea; **lata para ~** tea-caddy; **~-mate** (of herbal tea) maté; **~-paulista** tea-dance; ~ **preto** black tea; **salão de ~** tea-room; ~ **sem açúcar** tea without sugar; ~ **verde** green tea

chã *nf* round of beef

chacina *nf* minced pork; minced cured meat

chafarica *nf* pub; tavern; grocery

chaga *nf* indian cress; nasturtium; lark's heel

chairar *vt* (of knife) to sharpen

chaleira *nf* (of tea) kettle; urn

chama *nf* flame

chambão *nm* cheap beef

chaminé *nf* funnel

champanha (champanhe) *nm* champagne

champignon *nm* mushroom

chamuça *nf* samoosa; small savoury pastry

chamuscar *vt* to singe; to sear; to char; to scorch

chancarina (chancarona) *nf* sea fish: sea bream

chanfana *nf* liver stew; badly-cooked dish

chanfaneiro *nm* inn-keeper; cheap eatery owner

chantilly *nm* cream

chapa de aquecimento *nf* (of cooker &c) hot-plate

chapéu *nm* wine lees; **~-armado** sea fish: hammerhead shark; **~-de-chuva** umbrella; **~-de-cobra** (of mushroom) chanterelle; **~-de-sol** malabar almond; **~-velho** reheated, stale coffee

chaputa *nf* sea fish: sea bream

charcutaria (charcuteria) *nf* delicatessen; sausage retailer; meat chop

charcuteiro *nm* pork butcher; (of person) sausage-maker

charlota *nf* (of apple &c) charlotte

charneca *nf* Guinea pepper, red-pepper

charque *nm* jerked beef

charque-de-vento *nm* [Braz] wind-dried jerk

charquear *vt* (of meat) to jerk

charqueio *nm* beef-jerking

charutaria *nf* cigar shop; tobacconist

charutear *vi* to cigar-smoke

charuteira *nf* cigar-case

charuteiro *nm* sea fish: amberjack; cigar-shop owner; cigar manufacturer

charuto *nm* cigar; cheroot; honey/wine drink; cigar-shaped cake

chata *nf* funeral meal

chatobriã *nm* thick loin steak

chavão *nm* cake-mould;

decoration mould
chave *nf* key; light-switch
chávena *nf* tea-cup; cup
chaviano *a* black-pudding
chazeiro *a* tea-loving
chegar *vi* to arrive
cheia *nf* abundance
cheio *a* full-up, full; crammed; stuffed
cheiradeira *nf* snuff-box
cheirar *vt* to sniff, to smell
cheiro-verde *nm* (of bunch) parsley/spring onion
cheiros *nmpl* green spices; aromatic substances; **ramo de ~** bouquet garni
cheiroso *a* flavourous; fragrant; savoury
cheque *nm* (of money) cheque (check [USA])
cherna (cherne) (chernete) (chernote) *nm* sea fish: black grouper; stone bass; wreckfish
cherne *nm* sea fish: snowy grouper; **~-vermelho** sea fish: red snapper
chiba (chibato, chibo *nm) nf* (of goat) kid
chibé *nm* sweet cassava drink
chica *nf* strong herbed alcoholic drink; cigarette-end; meat; titbit; fermented maize/honey/nut drink
chícharo *nm* chick-pea
chicharro *nm* sea fish: saurel; horse mackerel
chicle *nm* chewing-gum
chicória *nf* chicory, endive
chila *nf* malabar gourd
chileno *nm* Chilean; [Braz] cattle breed
chilli *nm* chili pepper
chimarrão *nm* coffee/tea/maté served unsweetened
chimarrear *vi* [Braz] to drink unsweetened maté
chimarronear *vi* [Braz] to drink unsweetened maté
chinchar *vt* to dry on rack; to cheese-press
chinês *nm* chinese
chioba *nf* mutton-fish; abalone
chipa *nf* cheese doughnut
chique *a* smart; elegant; well-dressed
chiqueira *nf* teru-tero; plover variety
chirivia *nf* parsnip
chispe *nm* pig's trotter; edible entrails
chocho *a* tasteless; addled; (of sparkling wine) flat; *nm* mollusc: cuttlefish
chocolataria *nf* chocolate shop
chocolate *nm* chocolate; **~ quente** hot chocolate
chocolateira *nf* chocolate-pot; water-boiling container
chocolateiro *nm* chocolate-maker
chocorreta *nf* gulp of wine
chofer *nm* cab-driver
chope *nm* draught beer
chope-duplo *nm* double-sized mug of beer

choquinho *nm* small cuttlefish
chorão *nm* freshwater fish: catfish
chorolambre *nm* (of fish) small catfish
chorume *nm* lard; grease
chorumento *a* juicy; succulent
choupa *nf* black sea-bream
chouriça de vinhais *nf* spiced garlic-ed pork sausage
chouriçada *nf* string of sausages
chouriceiro *nm* (of person) sausage-maker
chouriço *nm* sausage; smoked sausage; black pudding; **~ de mel** honeyed sausage; **~ mouro** garlic/chili/spice/offal pork-sausage; **~ portalegre** smoked chili/garlic pork-sausage; **~ serrano** smoked chili/garlic pork-sausage
chuã *nm* fruit basket
chuchu *nm* (of fruit) chayote
chuchurrear *vi* to sip
chucrute *nm* sauerkraut
chufa *nf* (of confectionery) chufa-sedge-root sweet
chupeta *nf* (of drink) straw
chupita *nf* sea fish: caribe
churrascada *nf* (of dish/ assembly) barbecue
churrascaria *nf* rotisserie
churrasco *nm* barbecue; spit-roasted meat
churrasqueada *nf* barbecuing
churrasquear *vt* to barbecue
churrasqueira *nf* (of spit) barbecue
churrasqueiro *nm* barbecue-chef
churrasquinho *nm* [Braz] kebab
chuveiro *nm* shower
cíato *nm* wine ladle; liquid measure of 45ml approx
cica *nf* (of flavour) sharpness
cidra *nf* cider; (of fruit) citron; citron cider; crystallized citron rind
cidrada *nf* (of confectionery) crystallized citron rind sweet
cidrão *nm* (of jelly confectionery) citron rind sweet
cifa *nf* fish oil
cigarrar *vi* (of cigarettes) to smoke
cigarraria *nf* cigarette/tobacco shop
cigarreira *nf* cigar/cigarette-case
cigarreiro *(a) nm(f)* cigarette worker; tobacco variety
cigarrilha (cigarrinha) *nf* cigarillo; small inexpensive cigar
cigarro *nm* cigarette
cilindro de bicos *nm* (of roller) meat tenderizer
cima *nf* top
cinamomo *nm* cinnamon
cínara *nf* artichoke
cincho *nm* cheese mould; cylindrical cheese press
cinco *nm* (of number) five

cinzeiro *nm* ashtray
cioba *nf* sea fish: snapper
círculo *nm* circle
cirial *nm* chandelier
cisne *nm* swan
citráceo *nm* (of fruit) citrine
cítreo *a* citrus
cítrico *a* citrus; **ácido ~** citric acid
citrina *nf* lemon essence
clame *nm* clam; **sopa de ~** clam chowder
clara *nf* egg-white
clarete *nm* (of wine) claret
clarificar *vt* to clarify
claro *a* clear
classificação *nf* classification
classificar *vt* to classify; to grade; to assort
clúpeo *nm* (of fish) clupeoid; herring/sprat/anchovy family
coada *nf* strained vegetables
coador *nm* colander; filter; strainer; sieve; **~ chinês** piping-bag
coagulado *a* coagulated; curdled
coagulador *nm* rennet
coagular *vt/vi* to curdle; to clot; to thicken
coalha-leite *nf* (of artichoke) cardoon
coalhada *nf* curdled milk; curd
coalhado *a* curdled; off; sour
coalhar *vt* to curdle; to clot; to thicken
coalheira *nf* rennet, curd
coalho *nm* rennet; (of artichoke) cardoon
coar *vt* (of liquid) to strain
cobaia (porquinho-da-índia *nm) nf* guinea-pig
coberta *nf* (of table) cover; (of courses) menu
coberto *nm* verandah; *a* lidded; covered; (of food) coated
cobertor *nm* wrapper
cobertura *nm* wrapper; cover
cobra-do-mar *nf* sea fish: conger-eel
cobrado *nm* cover-charge
cobre *nm* copper
cobreira *nf* sugar-cane spirits
cobrir *vt* to cover; to coat; to spread; **~ com açúcar** to glaze
cobu *nm* banana-leaf biscuit
coca *nf* pumpkin; gourd
cocada *nf* (of confectionery) coconut sweet
cocção *nf* cooking; boiling; concoction
cochero *nf* cabby
cocho *nm* coconut; pig
coco *nm* coconut; cup; coconut-shell cup
coco-de-colher *nm* green coconut
cocotte *nm* (of eggs &c) individual (small) pan
côdea *nf* husk; hull; (of bread) crust
codeúdo *nm* crusty; crust-covered
codório *nm* sip of wine/brandy
codorniz (codorna) *nf* quail

codorno *nm* large pear variety
coelho (~a) *nm(f)* rabbit; **~ à caçadora** rabbit stewed in wine sauce
coentrada *nf* coriander sauce
coentro *nm* coriander
cogumelo *nm* (of mushroom) morel
coió *nm* (of fish) batfish
coita *nf* large kitchen knife
coité *nm* gourd cup
cola *nf* cola; **~ de peixe** isinglass
colação *nm* light meal; collation
colagem *nf* (of wine) clarifying
colar *vt* (of wine) to clarify; to stick
Colares *nm* wine-growing region
colarinho *nm* (of beer) head
colchão *nm* (of pastry) roly-poly
colesterol *nm* cholesterol
colheita *nf* vintage; harvest; crop
colher *nf* spoon; spoonful; ladle; **~ de chá** tea-spoon; caddy-spoon; **~ de pau** wooden spoon; **~ de sobremesa** dessert spoon; **~ de sopa** tablespoon; *vt* to harvest; to pick
colherada *nf* spoonful; ladleful
colherão *nm* ladle; large spoon; scoop
colhimento *nm* (of fruit &c) picking
colmeia *nf* beehive
colondro *nm* bottle gourd
colorau *nm* paprika
colza *nf* rape
combinar *vt* to mix-in; to combine; to add
comedor *nm* (of person) diner
comer *nm* meal; *vt* to eat; to swallow; to chew; **~ fora de casa** to eat out
comes *nmpl* food
comestível *nm/f* food; cosmestibles; *a* cosmestible; eatable
comezinho *a* eatable; appetizing
comida *nf* food; meal; cuisine; eating; **~ pesada** stodgy food; **~ por quilo** self-service; **~ simples** simple fare; plain diet; **~ vegetariana** veggie food; **~ para viagem** takeaway
comido *a* eaten; swallowed
cominho *nm* cumin
cominho-armênio *nm* caraway seeds
comissária de bordo *nf* (of aircraft) stewardess
comível *a* eatable; edible
complemento *nm* complement; accompaniment
comportar *vt* (of price &c) to include
compota *nf* (of fruit &c) compote; jam
compra *nf* purchase
comprar *vt* to buy; to purchase; **~ a crédito** to buy on credit

compreendido *a* included
comprimir *vt* to squash; to compress
comua *nf* WC
conca *nf* porringer; small bowl
concentração *nf* (of liquid &c) concentration
concentrado *nm* (of liquid &c) concentration; essence
concha *nf* shell; ladle; scoop
conchada *nf* ladleful; scoopful
conchado (concheado) *a* shell-shaped
condensar *vt* to condense
condimentação *nf* seasoning
condimentado *a* seasoned; spicy
condimentar *vt* to season; to spice
condimento *nm* seasoning; spice; condiment; dressing
condir *vt* to season; to spice
condutar *vt* (of accompaniment) to eat bread
conduto *nm* bread-accompanied food
confecção *nf* (of recipe) method
confeccionador *a* confectionery
confeiçoar *vt* (of confectionery/pâtisseries) to make; to prepare
confeitada *nf* Easter cake
confeitado *a* (of fruit) crystallized
confeitar *vt* (of confectionery/pâtisseries) to make; to prepare
confeitaria *nf* (of confectionery/pâtisseries) sweet-shop
confeiteira *nf* (of confectionery) serving-dish
confeiteiro (a) *nm(f)* confectioner
confeito *nm* confection, sweet
confete *nm* (of wedding) confetti
congelado *a* frozen
congelador *nm* freezer; *a* freezing
congelamento *nm* (of food) freezing
congelar *vt* to freeze; to ice; to chill; **~ a vácuo** freeze-dry
congestionamento *nm* (of traffic) congestion
congro *nm* sea fish: conger-eel
conhaque *nm* cognac; brandy
conquilha *nf* conch
conserva *nf* conserve; preserve; comfit; **em ~** canned; pickled; **~s** canned goods
conserveiro *nm* (of person) canner; confectioner
consistência *nf* consistency; firmness
consistente *a* consistent; thick; solid
consoada *nf* light supper
consoar *vi* to sup lightly
consomê *nm* consommé
consumação *nm* cover charge
consumir *vt* to eat; to consume

consumível *a* consumable
conta *nf* (of restaurant) bill; **~-minutos** *nm* egg-timer
contado *a* counted; **de ~** ready cash
contente *a* content; happy
conter *vt* to contain
conteúdo *nm* (of container) contents; (of alcohol) strength
contrafilé *nm* [Braz] sirloin
conúbio *nm* marriage; wedding
convescote *nm* picnic
convir *vi* to complement each other
convival *a* convivial
copa *nf* pressing-vat; pantry
copada *nf* cupful; glassful
coparrão *nm* large-cupful
copázio *nm* large glass(ful)
copeira *nf* waitress; cupboard; side-board; pantry
copeiragem *nf* [Braz] butlering
copeirar *vi* to butler
copeiro (a) *nm(f)* butler, (butleress)
copiar *nm* verandah; porch
copo *nm* cup(ful); glass(ful); tumbler(ful); **~-d'água** snack; **~ alto** (of glass) highball
copra *nf* copra; dried coconut kernel
copraol *nm* coconut oil, copra oil
coque *nm* chef, cook
coquetel *nm* cocktail; **~ de camarão** shrimp cocktail; **~ de lagosta** lobster cocktail
coqueteleira *nf* cocktail-shaker
coquilho *nm* palm-nut kernels
coquinho *nm* small coconut
cor *nf* colour
coração *nm* [Braz] large room; verandah; (of apple &c) core; **~-de-boi** custard apple; **~-de-rainha** cherimoya fruit
coral (corais *pl)* *nm* (of scallops &c) coral
corantes alimentares *nmpl* food-colouring
corbelha *nf* (of confectionery/ fruit/flowers) small basket
corço (~a) *nm(f)* roe deer (doe)
corda *nf* sinew; string
cordeira *nf* ewe lamb; **~ assado** roast lamb; **costelete de ~** lamb chop
cordeirinho *nm* small lamb
cordial *nm* cordial; refreshing drink
coregono *nm* freshwater herring; pollan; **~ branco** freshwater whitefish; vendace
coriandro *nm* coriander
corindiba (corindiúba) *nf* hackberry
corinto *nm* currant; raisin
cornetinha *nf* conch
cornicabra *nf* capisicum; chili pepper
cornicabra-dos-algarvios *nf* (of fruit) sea grape
cornimboque *nm* horn tobacco box
cornisolo *nm* (of fruit) dogberry; wild gooseberry

cornucópia *nf* cornucopia; horn of plenty; abundance
cornuda *nf* hammerhead shark
coroa *nf* crown
coroado *nm* sparrow variety
cororô *nm* (of cooking pot) scorched rice
corote *nm* small cask
corpo *nm* (of animal) body; **vinho de ~** full-bodied wine
corredura *nf* residual liquid in emptied vessel
corrente *a* (of water) running
corrupio *nm* [Braz] sea urchin
corta-bainha (cachaça) *nf* white rum
corta-charutos *nm* cigar-cutter
corta-massa *nm* (of shapes) pastry-cutter
cortadeira *nf* pastry cutter
cortadora *nf* bacon-slicer
cortar *vt* to cut; to trim; to mince; **~ em cubos** to dice; to carve; (of tap) to turn-off; (of wine &c) to adulterate
corte *nm* (of knife) cutting-edge; cut; (of cattle) slaughtering; *nf* slaughterhouse
corvina *nf* sea (freshwater **pescada)** fish: corvina; croaker
corvo *nm* raven; crow
coscorão *nm* omelette; fritter; pancake
cosmestível *a* cosmestible
costado *nm* (of beef &c) flank
costas *nfpl* back
costela *nf* (of meat) rib; chop
costeleta *nf* chop; cutlet; (of fish) steak; **de boi** beef entrecôte; **~ de borrego (~ de carneiro)** lamb chop; **~ de porco** pork chop; **~ de vitela** veal chop
costilhar *nm* (of beef) roast(ing) rib
cotão *nm* (of peach-skin &c) down; fluff
cotio *a* chick-pea
cotó *nm* [Braz] small knife
cotovia *nf* lark, sky lark
cotréia *nf* [Braz] cheap white rum
couraçado *nm* sea fish: armoured catfish
courato *nm* pork skin; rind
couve *nf* cabbage; spring greens; kale; collard greens; **~-brócolos** broccoli; **~-de-bruxelas** Brussels sprout; **~-flor** cauliflower; **~ galega** kale; **~ lombarda** white cabbage; **~ marroquina** red cabbage; **~-nabo** swede; **~-rábano** kohlrabi; **~ repolhuda** cabbage; **~ vermelha** red cabbage
covilhete *nm* (of presentation) cake-dish; sweets-plate
coxa *nf* thigh
coxinhas *nfpl* [Braz] deep-fried chicken hors d'oeuvre
cozedura *nf* cooking; cookery; baking; boiling; food; (of soup) chunky bits

cozer *vt* to cook; (of bread &c) to bake; to boil
cozido *a* cooked; baked; boiled; *nm* beef/potato/cabbage stew; **~ à portuguesa** rice/vegetables/beans/meat casserole
cozimento *nm* cooking; baking; boiling
cozinha *nf* kitchen; cuisine; cookery; (of dishes) preparation; **~ de campanha** field kitchen; **~ de navio** (of ship) galley
cozinhado *nm* cooked food
cozinhador *nm* chef; cook
cozinhar *vt* to cook; to bake; to boil; to simmer; to stew
cozinheira *nf* cook
cozinheiro (~a) *nm(f)* cook; **~ chefe** chef
craca *nf* goose barnacle
cravinho (cravo-da-índia) *nm* (of spice) clove
cravo-do-maranhão *nm* [Braz] (of spice) clove cinnamon; clove of Maramhan
creche *nf* crèche
crédito *nm* credit
creme *nm* cream; custard; **~ coalhado** clotted cream; **~ de leite** double-cream; heavy cream [USA]; **~ de leite azedo** sour cream; **~de limão** lemon curd; **~ de milho** white-sauced sweetcorn; **~ de papaya** creamed cassised papaya; **queijo ~** cream-cheese
cremor de tártaro *nm* cream of tartar
cremoso *a* creamy
crepe *nm* crêpe
crescer *vi* to grow; to shoot; to sprout
creta *nf* sea fennel, samphire
cria *nf* (of pig &c) suckling; calf; (of goat) kid; **gado de ~** young cattle
criação *nf* poultry; cattle
criada *nf* maid; **~ de cozinha** kitchen-maid
criado (~a) *nm(f)* servant; **~ (~a) de mesa** waiter(ress); **~-mudo** dumb-waiter
criança *nf* child
criatório *nm* [Braz] cattle; cattle farm
cricifera *nf* cabbage variety
crioulo *nm* maize-leaf-covered cigarette; *a* Creole; spicy
crista *nf* cockscomb
cristal *nm* (of glass) crystal
cristalizado *a* (of fruit) crystallized
crivo *nm* colander; sieve; strainer; skimmer
crocante *a* crunchy
crocodilo *nm* crocodile
croquete *nm* croquette; meat (&c)-ball
crosta *nf* crust; rind; skin
cru *a* raw; uncooked; unprocessed
cruá (melão-caboclo *nm)* *nf* cassbanana, musk cucumber

crusta (crosta) *nf* crust; rind; skin
crustáceo *nm* crustacean
cruz *nf* cross
cruza *nf* (of breeding) cross
cuba *nf* cask; tub; vat; (of wine) Alentejo vineyard
cubeba *nf* (of spice) cubeb pepper
cubinho *nm* small cube
cubo *nm* cube
cuca (cuque) *nf* chef; cook; (of food) cake
cucharra *nf* [Braz] wooden spoon
cucurbitáceo (cucurbitino) *a* gourd-like
cuí *nm* sifted flour; tobacco dust
cuia *nf* bottle gourd; maté gourd cup
cuiada *nf* [Braz] gourdful of maté
cuiambuca (cumbuca) *nf* [Braz] gourd bottle
cuiapitinga *nf* [Braz] black gourd vessel
cuidado *nm* care; take care!
cuietê (cuité) *nm/f* [Braz] bottle gourd
cuim *nm* [Braz] rice chaff
cuinhira ([Braz] **crueira)** *nf* cassava flour residue
cuité ([Braz] **coité)** *nm/f* bottle gourd
cuiu-cuiu (armado) (armao) (abotoado) *nm* freshwater catfish
cuiuíra ([Braz] **crueira)** *nf* cassava flour residue
cujuba *nf* small gourd cup
culape *nm* (of meat/bread &c) large chunk
culinária *nf* cookery
culinário *a* culinary
cultivar *vt* to grow
cultivo *nm* cultivation
cumari (cumarim) *nm* [Braz] chili, goat pepper
cumbaca (anujá) *nf* [Braz] freshwater fish: catfish
cumprimentar *vt* to greet; (of chef) to compliment
cunandatiá *nf* [Braz] hyacinth bean, lablab
cupu *nm* cacao bean-type fruit/drink
cupuaçu *nm* cacao bean-type fruit
cuque ([Braz] **cuca)** *nm* cake
curaçau *nm* (of liqueur) curaçao
curadá *nm* chestnut/tapioca cake
curado *a* smoked; cured; sun-dried; (of cheese) hardened
cural *nm* grated caramel-ed sweetcorn
curar *vt* to cure; to sun-dry; (of cheese) to harden; to preserve
curau *nm* [Braz] cassava-ed salt-meat
curera *nf* cassava (manioc) pulp
curimã *nm* [Braz] sea fish: striped mullet

curimbatá (curimatã) (curimatá) (curimba) (papa-terra) *nm* [Braz] Amazon scale fish
curso *nm* (of cookery-school &c) course
curtimento *nm* pickling
curtir *vt* to pickle olives
curuatá-açu *nm* agave
curupiá *nf* [Braz] hackberry
cuscuz *nm* [Braz] couscous; **~ paulista** fish/maize-flour couscous
cuscuzeira *nf* [Braz] couscous kettle
cuspidor *nm* spittoon
custar *vi* to cost; **~ caro** to cost a lot
custo (~a) *nm(f)* cost
custoso *a* expensive
cutela *nf* (of butcher) cleaver
cutelaria *nf* cutlery
cuteleiro *nm* cutler
cutelo *nm* mezzaluna; chopping-knife
cutilão *nm* large chopping-knife
cutipaca ([Braz] **cavaleiro)** *nf* prawn
cuxá *nm* ginger/vinegar sauce

D

daiquiri *nm* daiquiri, rum-based cocktail
damasco *nm* damson; damson plum; apricot
dança *nf* dance
dandá *nm* [Braz] chufa, nut-grass tuba
Dão *nm* wine-growing region
data *nf* (of time) date; **~ de nascimento** birthday
datil *nm* (of palm) date
debicar *vt* to sample; to try; to nibble
decantação *nf* decanting
decantador *nm* decanter
decantar *vt* to decant
decocção *nm* decoction; reduction; boiling
dedo *nm* finger
defeso (defesso) *a* prohibited
defesso *nm* (of fishing/ hunting) close(d) season
defumação *nm* (of fish/meat) smoking; curing
defumado *a* (of fish/meat) smoked; cured
defumadouro *nm* smokery
defumadura *nm* smoking; curing
defumar *vt* (of fish/meat) to smoke; to cure; **arenque (salgado e) ~ado** kipper
degelar *vt* to thaw; to defrost
degelo *nm* thawing; defrosting
degustação *a* tasting; **~ de vinhos** wine tasting
deitar *vt* to pour; to spill
deixar *vt* to leave; (of cooking) to set aside
delfim *nm* dolphin
delibação *nf* sampling; tasting; sipping
delibar *vt* to sample; to taste; to sip

delicia *nf* delicacy
delicioso *a* delicious
demais *a* too much
demolhar *vt* to soak in water
dendê *nm* African palm oil
denominação *nm* denomination; appellation; **~ de origem protegida** (d.o.p.) (of origin) exclusive legal name denoting a standard
densidade (densidão) *nf* density
dente *nm* tooth; (of fork) prong; (of garlic) clove; **al ~** (of consistency) crunchy
dente-de-leão *nm* dandelion
denteado *a* tooth-patterned; (of knife) serrated
dentilha *nf* sea fish: cuckoo wrasse
depósito *nm* dregs; sediment
derrancar *vi* to turn rancid; to go off
derretedura *nf* melting
derreter *vt* to melt
derretido *a* melted
desafaimar *vi* to assuage hunger
desarrolhamento *nm* corkage
desarrolhar *vt* to uncork
desataviado *a* ungarnished
desbagoar *vt* to pick grapes from cluster
desbagulhar *vt* (of fruit) to pick-out seeds
desbeiçar *vt* (of glass &c) to chip
desborrar *vt* (of wine &c) to remove dregs
desbulhar *vt* to shell; to peel
descabeçar *vt* (of fish) to head
descaída *nf* chicken pluck
descamisar *vt* to husk
descansador (descanso) *nm* (of glass &c) coaster; mat
descaroçador *nm* (of fruit) stoning-machine; coring-machine
descaroçar *vt* (of fruit) to stone; to core
descarolar *vt* (of apple &c) to core
descascação (descasque *nm) nf* peel; shell; husk
descascador *nm* peeler; husker
descascar *vt* to peel; to husk; to skin
descer *vt* (of staircase) to descend
descodear *vt* (of bread) to decrust
descongelação *nf* defrosting
descongelar *vt* to thaw; to defrost
desconto *nm* (of money) discount
descoraçar *vt* to de-core
descorticar *vt* to shell; to peel
descremação *nf* (of milk) to skim off the cream
descremar *vt* (of cream) to skim
desejar *vt* (of pregnant women) to crave
desempanar *vt* (of glass &c)

to wipe

desemplumar *vt* (of feathers) to pluck

desencascar *vt* to de-cask

desenfornar *vt* to remove from oven

desenfrascar *vt* (of bottle/ flask) to pour out

desengaçar *vt* to gobble

desengarrafar *vt* (of bottle) to pour

desengordurar *vt* (of fat &c) to skim-off

desenjoativo *nm* aperitif; appetizer; *a* delicious; tasty; appetizing

desfastio *nm* appetite

desfazer *vi* (of butter &c) to melt

desfeita (desfeito *nm) nf* cod/ onion/chickpea dish

desfeito *a* (of butter &c) melted; diluted; dissolved

desfiar *vt* to fillet; to shred; to slice thinly

desfolhada *nf* (of maize &c) husking

desfruta *nf* [Braz] coconut harvest

desfrutar *vt* (of fruit) to pick

desinfetante *nm* disinfectant

desistir *vt* (of smoking &c) to give up

desjejua (desjejum) *nf* breaking fast

desjejuar *vt* to break fast

deslaçado *a* (of liquids/solids emulsions) separated

deslassar *vt* to dilute

desmiolar *vt* (of loaf) remove soft centre

desnatação *nf* (of milk) creaming; skimming

desnatadeira *nf* (of milk) skimmer; creamer

desnatar *vt* (of milk) to cream; to skim

desossado *a* (of meat) boned

desossar *vt* (of meat) to bone

desparafusar *vt* to unscrew

despedida *nf* (of dinner) farewell

despejamento *nm* spilling; decanting

despejar *vt* to pour; to decant; to empty; to spill

despejo *nm* spilling; pouring out

despencar *vt* [Braz] (of grapes &c) to remove from bunch

despender *vt* (of money) to spend

despensa *nf* pantry; larder; storeroom; buttery

despenseiro *nm* cellarman; steward; butler

despesa *nf* cost; charge; **~s adicionais (~ extras) (~ suplementares)** supplementary charge

desplumar *vt* (of feathers) to pluck

despojos *nmpl* left-overs

despolpar *vt* to pulp; (of coffee) to hull

desrolhar *vt* (of bottle) to open; to uncork

dessabor *nm* tastelessness; flavourlessness
dessaborido (dessaboroso) *a* tasteless; insipid
dessalgado *a* insipid; unsalted
dessalgar *vt* (of salt removal) to soak
dessazonado *a* unripe; unseasoned
dessecação *nf* desiccation
dessecar *vt* to desiccate
dessedentar *vt* (of thirst) to quench
destampar *vt* to open
destapar *vt* (of bottle) to open; to uncork; to uncover; (of champagne &c) to crack
destemperar *vt* (of wine &c) to dilute; to reduce temperature
destilação *nf* distillation; distillery
destilador *nm* (of person) distiller; (of alcohol) still
destilar *vt* to distil
destilaria *nf* distillery
destorcedor *nm* [Braz] sugar-cane press
detergente *nm* detergent
deteriorável *a* perishable
devorar *vt* devour
dextrose *nf* dextrose; corn sugar
dez *nm* (of number) ten
dezembro *nm* December
dia *nm* day; **~ de abstinência (~ de jejum)** fast day; **~ de ano novo** New Year's Day; **~ de anos** birthday; **bons ~s!** good morning!; **~ de carne** meat day; **~ feriado** holiday; **~ de natal** Christmas day; **neste ~** today; **~ santo (~ do Senhor)** Sunday; holiday; **~ de semana** weekday
diabético *a* diabetic
diabo-marinho (tamboril) *nm* sea fish: angler
diacidrão *nm* (of confectionery) lemon-peel sweet
diacódio *nm* white poppy syrup
dieta (dietético) *nf* diet; **fazer ~** to diet
digestivo *nm* (of alcohol) digestif; post-prandial spirits
diluir *vt* to dilute
diluto *a* dilute; [Braz] (of wine &c) with-water
dinheiro *nm* money; cash
dioscoreácea *nf* chinese/ japanese yam
diospireiro *nm* (of tree) persimmon
direito *nm* tax; (of customs) duty
discurso *nm* (of oration) speech
dispêndio *nm* expenditure
dissolver *vt* to dissolve
dividir *vt* to apportion
dobrada *nf* stomach of cow/ calf
dobradinha *nm* [Braz] tripe/ beans/sausage/tomatoes stew

doçaria *nf* (of confectionery) sweet-shop
doce *nm* (of confectionery) sweet; **~ de passas** currant-bun; *a* sweet; **~-de-pimenta** [Braz] black-pepper/cassava/sugar cake
doceiro *nm* confectioner
doçura *nf* sweetness; sugariness
dois *nm* (of number) two
dólar *nm* dollar
doméstico *nm* (of servant) domestic
domingo *nm* Sunday
domínio *nm* domaine
dona-branca *nf* [Braz] white rum; spirits
doninha *nf* dolphin; sea lamprey
donut *nm* doughnut
donzela *nf* freshwater fish: burbot; ling
d.o.p. (denominação de origem protegida) *abbr* (of origin) exclusive name denoting a legal standard
dorada (sardinhão) (apapá) *nm* [Braz] freshwater fish: Amazonian herring
dormitório *nm* bedroom; **corro ~** (of train) sleeping-car
dorna *nf* vat
dorso *nm* back
dourada (doirada) *nf* [Braz] dory, gilthead; **~ de mar** sea bream
douradinha (doiradinha) *nf* golden plover
dourado (doirado) *nm* [Braz] freshwater fish: dorado, dolphin fish; **~-do-mar** sea fish: dolphin; **~-branco (tabarana) (tubarana)** freshwater fish: tabarana
dourar *vt* to glaze; to fry; to toast
Douro *nm* Douro river; port/wine-growing district
doze *nm* (of number) twelve
dozena *nf* dozen
drope *nm* (of confectionery) drop
drupa *nf* (of fruit) stone
duas *nf* (of number) two
ducha *nf* shower
dulcificação *nf* sweetening
dulcificado *a* sweetened
dulcificar *vt* to sweeten
dulcífico *a* sweet
dundu *nm* [Braz] freshwater fish: catfish
durasno *nm* peach
duro *a* (of cheese &c) hard
duro-a-fogo *nm* cheap tobacco
dúzia *nf* dozen

E

ebó (ebô) *nm* [Braz] corn/dendê-oil dish
ebulição *nf* boiling; **ponto de ~** boiling-point
ebuliente *a* boiling
ebulir *vt* to boil
econômico *a* inexpensive; cheap

ecônomo *nm* steward; pantryman
edulcorar *vt* to sweeten
édulo *a* edible; eatable
efervescente *a* fizzy
efó *nm* [Braz] dendê-oil/shrimp/vegetable dish
eglefim *nm* sea fish: haddock
égrio *nm* nasturtium
eiró (enguia *nf) nm* eel
eiroz *nm* conger eel
eiva *nf* (of fruit) blemish
eivar *vi* (of fruit) to go bad
elevador (ascensor) *nm* lift; elevator; **~ de serviço** service lift
elixir *nm* elixir
ema *nf* rhea
emassar *vt* to make into a paste
embamata *nf* roux
embarricar (embarrilar) *vt* to barrel
embeber *vt/vi* to imbibe; to soak
embetara (betara) (papa-terra) *nf* sea fish: southern kingfish
emboca *nm* (of party) gate-crasher
emborcar *vt* to empty; to drain (-off); to pour
embotijar *vt* to bottle/jug
embriagador *a* intoxicating
embuchado *a* well-fed
emelar *vt* to sweeten; to honey
ementa *nf* menu
emostar *vt* to ripen; to sweeten; (of fermentation) to must
empachado *a* sated
empaçocar *vt* [Braz] to fill up with paçoca (cassava-ed fried meat)
empada *nf* pasty
empanada *nf* large pasty/pie
empanar *vt* to bread; *a* breaded
empanzinamento *nm* glut
empapelar *vt* to paper-wrap
empastatriz *nf* (of implement) mixer; kneader
empelo *nm* bread dough-lump; sieved vegetable
empencado *a* [Braz] (of grapes &c) clustered
empetro *nm* (of plant) crowberry
empregada *nf* maid
emulsionar *vt* to emulsify; to mix liquids
emulsivo *a* (of nuts &c) emulsive; oil-producing
encachaçar-se *vi* to get tight on sugar-cane brandy
encalir *vt* to brown; to par-boil
encandilar *vt* (of fruit &c) to crystallize
encaracolar *vt* to twist; to spiral
encaramelar *vt* to caramel
encarnado *a* (of peppers &c) red
encarrascar-se *vi* to get drunk on plonk
encarraspanar-se *vi* to get drunk
encharcar *vt* to soak

enchedeira *nf* (of implement) filler; funnel
encher *vt* (of glass &c) to fill
enchido *nm* sausage; stuffing
enchimento *nm* (of poultry &c) stuffing, forcemeat
enchouriçar (enchoiriçar) *vi* to make sausage-shaped
enchova *nf* sea fish: anchovy; blue fish; tailor
encilhadela *nf* maté top-up
encodeamento *nm* (of bread) crust; crusting; husk
encodear *vt* to crust; **~-se** to form a crust
encomendar *vt* (of restaurant) to order
encorpado *a* (of wine) full-bodied
encrostar *vt/vi* to crust
encruar *vt* to half/under-cook
encubação *nf* (of wine &c) vatting
encubar *nf* (of wine &c) to vat
endivía *nf* endive; chicory
endomingado *a* Sunday best; elegant
endrão *nm* wild dill
endro *nm* dill
enequim *nm* large shark
enfarelar *vt* to bran
enfarinhadela *nf* flour-sprinkling/covering
enfarinhado (farinhento) (farinhoso) *a* floury
enfarinhar *vt* to flour; to dust; to powder
enfeite *nm* garnish
enformar *vt* (of mould) to shape
enfornar *vt* to place in oven
enfrascar *vt* to bottle
enfunilamento *nm* (of liquids &c) funnelling
enfunilar *vt* (of liquids &c) to funnel; to make funnel-shaped
engaço *nm* (of bunch of grapes) stalk; husk
engarafado *a* (of contents) bottled
engarapar *vi* [Braz] to give garapa (sugar-cane juice)
engordar *vt* (of livestock) to fatten
engrolar *vt* to par-boil
engrossante *nm* baby-food
engrossar *vt* to thicken
enguia (eiró) *nf* eel; **~ marinha** conger-eel
engulosinar *vi* to whet the appetite; (of confectionery) to gain liking for sweets
engunhar *vi* (of fruit) to wither
enho *nm* young deer
enlatado *a* (of fruit &c) tinned, canned
enlatar *vt* (of fruit &c) to tin, to can
enofilia *nf* oenophilia; love-of-wine
enologia *nf* oenology; knowledge/study of wines
enomel *nm* wine/honey drink
enômetro *nm* oenometer; wine-alcohol tester
ensaboar *vt* to soap

ensalmourar (ensalmoirar) *vt* to brine
ensolarado *a* sunned, sunny
ensopado *nm* stew; ragout; (of fish) chowder
ensopar *vt* to stew; to soak; to douse
entalar *vt* to (of preservation) to quick-fry
entrada *nf* (of dish) starter; appetizer; entrée; (of building) entrance; entry; **~ proibida** no entry
entrar *vt* to enter
entrecosto *nm* (of beef &c) rib
entrecozer *vt* to parboil
entrega *nf* (of shopping) delivery
entremaduro *a* half-ripe
entremeado *a* (of bacon) streaky
entremear *vt* to mix-in
entreperna *nf* roasting/barbecuing-meat; (of dish) roast; barbecue
entrita *nf* panada; flavoured pulped bread
entuchar *vt* [Braz] to swallow down
envasilhar *vt* to bottle; to jar
envelhecimento *nm* (of port &c) ageing
envinagrado *a* vinegar-ed; vinegary
envinagrar *vt* to vinegar
envolver *vt* (of mixing) to fold-in; to cover
enxerçar *vt* (of meat) to salt and dry
enxova preta *nf* oil-fish
enxugar *vt* (of meat) to dry; (of liquid) to reduce; (of bottle) to empty
enxundiar *vt* (of animals) to fatten
enxundioso *a* (of animals) fatty; greasy; oily
epicurista *nm/f* epicure
épulas *nfpl* mouth-watering food
equipamento *nm* equipment
eremita-bernardo *nm* hermit-crab
eruca (arugula) *nf* (of herb) rocket
erva *nf* herb; **~-cidreira (~ melissa)** lemon balm; **~-doce** fennel; anise; **~-mate** (of herbal beverage) maté
ervagem *nf* vegetables; greens
ervanaria *nf* (of shop) herbalist
ervanário *nm* (of shop) herbalist
ervateiro *nm* maté seller
ervilha *nf* pea; pea-pod
esbagoar *vi* to pick (grapes) from bunch
esburgar *vt* to peel; to skin; to husk; to shell; (of bones) to pick
escabeche *nm* oil/vinegar/spice marinade; **~ de cavalinha** soused mackerel
escabulhar *vt* to peel; to skin; to husk; to shell
escabulho *nm* peel; husk

escada *nf* stairs; ~ **salva-vidas** emergency stairs; ~ **de serviço** back-stairs
escádea *nf* segment of grapes
escalda *nf* piquant sauce
escaldar *vt* (of vegetables) to blanch
escalfar *vt* to simmer; (of egg) to poach; (of dishes) to rinse; (of kitchen water) to heat
escalo *nm* freshwater fish: orfe, ide
escalope *nm* escalope; cutlet [USA]
escalrichado *a* tasteless; unsalted
escama *nf* (of fish) scale
escamação (escamadura) *nf* (of fish) scaling
escamado *a* (of fish) scaled
escamar *vt* (of fish) scale
escamudo *nm* sea fish: saithe; pollack; coley; rock-salmon
escanção *nm* wine-waiter/ server
escançar *vt* to pour the wine
escândea *nf* durum wheat
escangalhado *a* (of equipment) out of order
escaro *nm* sea fish: parrot-fish
escarola *nf* endive; chicory
escarradeira (escarradura) *nf* (of wine-tasting) spittoon
escoadura *nf* sediment, lees, dregs
escoar *vt* to drain-off; to decant; to empty; *vi* to leak
escodear *vt* (of bread) to remove crust
escola *nf* (of cookery) school
escorralhas *nfpl* dregs; lees
escorredor *nm* strainer; colander
escorrer *vt* to drain
escova *nf* brush; ~ **de mesa** crumb-brush; ~ **de roupa** clothes-brush
escudela *nf* wood porringer
esculento *a* edible
escuma *nf* froth
escumadeira *nf* skimmer
escumar *vt* to skim
escumoso *a* frothy; foamy
escuro *a* (of chocolate) dark
esfarelar *vt* to crumble
esfarinhado *a* crumbled
esfarinhar *vt* to crumble
esfatiar *vt* to slice
esfiha *nf* mincemeat-filled dough
esfirena (bicuda) *nf* sea fish: barracuda
esfomeação *nf* hungriness
esfomeado *a* hungry
esfriadouro *nm* (of wine) cooler
esfriamento *nm* refrigeration
esfriar *vt* to cool; to chill; to refrigerate; to freeze
esmagamento *nm* (of fruit) bruising; blemish
esmagar *vt* (of garlic &c) to crush
esmigalhar (migalhar) *vt* to crumble
esmiolar *vt* to crumb

esmorraçar (esmorrar) *vt* (of candle) to extinguish; to snuff-out
espaço *nm* space; room
espada *nf* sea fish: sword-fish
espadarte *nm* sea fish: sword-fish; **~-serra** sea-fish: sawfish
espadilha *nf* sea fish: sprat
espadim *nm* sea fish: marlin; **~-azul** blue marlin
espaguete *nm* spaghetti; **à bolonhesa** meat sauced; **~ com vôngole** vongole sauced
espalhar *vt* (of butter &c) to spread
espanada *nf* (of fish) fin
espanador *nm* feather duster; duster
espanar *vt* to dust
espanhol *nm* Spaniard
espargo *nm* asparagus
esparideos *nm* sea bream
esparregado *nm* dressed herbs; diced green vegetable stew
esparregar *vt* to prepare as a vegetarian dish
espátula *nf* spatula; freshwater fish: paddlefish
especialidade *nf* speciality
especiaria (espécia) *nf* spices; flavouring
especieiro *nm* spice-seller
espelho *nm* mirror
espelta *nf* (of wheat) spelt
esperar *vt* to await
esperlano *nm* (of fish) smelt
espessar *vt* to thicken
espetada *nf* skewer; **~s** wine/garlic-marinated kebabs
espeto *nm* (of roasting) spit
espevitado *a* (of candle) snuffed
espevitar *vt* (of candle) to snuff-out
espicha *nf* string of fish
espiga *nf* ear of corn; **~ de milho** corn-cob
espinafre *nm* spinach
espinha (espinhaço *nm) nf* (of fish &c) backbone, spine, bone; **sem ~s** (of fish &c) boneless
espinheiro-da-virgínia *nm* honey-locust; **~-preto** haw
espiral *a* (of pasta &c) spiral
espírito *nm* spirits; alcohol
espirituoso *a* alcoholic
esponjoso *a* spongy
espório *nm* spore
espreguiçadeira *nf* deck-chair
espremedor *nm* squeezer; (of potatoes &c) masher
espremedura *nf* squeezing; mashing
espremer *vt* to squeeze; (of potatoes &c) to mash; to compress
espuma *nf* (of beer &c) froth
espumadeira *nf* skimmer
espumante *a* (of wine) sparkling; bubbly; fizzy
espumar *vt* to skim; *vi* to bubble; to froth

espúmeo (espumífero) *a* bubbling; frothing
esqualo *nm* sea fish: shark
esquilo *nm* squirrel
essência *nf* essence; extract
estacionamento *nm* (of vehicle) parking; **~ proibido** no parking
estacionar *vt* (of vehicle) to park
Estados Unidos da América *nmpl* United States of America
estalajadeiro *nm* innkeeper
estalar *vt* to break; to break-up
estância *nf* estate; farm
estanhado *a* (of pan &c) tinned, tin-plated
estanho *nm* (of metal) tin
estável *a* (of temperature &c) steady; stable
estender *vt* to spread
esterilizar *vt* to sterilize
esterno *nm* breast-bone
estômago *nm* stomach
estragão *nm* tarragon
estreladeira *nf* egg-poaching pan
estrelado *a* (of egg) fried
estribeiro *nm* semi-soft ewe's milk cheese
estrombo *nm* conch
estropalho *nm* dishcloth
estrugir *vt* (of onions &c) to sweat; to cook until transparent
estufa *nf* stove; (of plants) greenhouse
estufadeira *nf* stew-pot/pan
estufado *nf* (of meat) stew; *a* stewed
estufar *vt* to stew; (of hare) to jug
esturjão *nm* sturgeon
esturro *nm* (of coffee &c) roasting
esvaziar *vt* (of bottle &c) to empty
etiqueta *nf* etiquette
EUA (Estados Unidos da América do Norte) *nmpl* USA
eucalipto *nm* eucalyptus
evaporado *a* evaporated
évora *nm* ewe's milk cheese
examinar *vt* to test; to try; to inspect
excedente *nm* residue; excess; surplus
exclusivo *a* exclusive
exorbitante *a* (of price &c) exorbitant; excessive; fancy
expiração *nf* expiry
exportação *nf* export
exportar *vt* to export
expresso *nm* espresso
extintor de incêndio *nm* fire-extinguisher
extracto *nm* extract
extrair *vt* to extract
extrato (extracto) *nm* extract; essence; **~ de carne** extract of beef

F

fabagela *nf* bean-caper

fábrica *nf* factory; mill; (of milk &c) dairy; (of sugar) refinery
fabricante *nm/f* maker; producer; (of beer) brewer
faca *nf* knife; **~s** cutlery; **~ de cozinha** kitchen-knife; **~ para peixe** fish-slice; **~ de trinchar** carving-knife
facão *nm* large knife; cleaver
facultativo *a* optional
fagópiro *nm* buckwheat
faisão *nm* pheasant
falerno *nm* good wine; Falernian wine
falha *nf* thin slice
falhar *vt* to slice-up thinly
falsificar *vt* (of drink) to spike
falso-alcaparreiro *nm* bean caper
faltar *vt* (of supplies) to go short of
faminto (famulento) *a* hungry; famished; peckish
faneca *nf* sea fish: pout; bib; piece of bread
fanecão *nm* sea fish: poor-cod
faneco *nm* bread; piece of bread; slice of bread
faqueiro *nm* (of cutlery/knives) canteen case
farauta *nf* old ewe
fardel *nm* lunch-box; pack-lunch
fareláceo *a* farinaceous; bran-like
farelento *a* high in bran
farelo *nm* bran
farinha *nf* flour; breadstuff; **~-d'água** fermented-cassava flour; **~ de cevada** barley-meal; **~ integral** wholemeal; **~-do-reino** *nf* wheat-flour; **~ de rosca** breadcrumbs
farinheira *nf* garlic/flour/chili sausage
farinheiro *a* farinaceous; floury
farinhento (farinhoso) *a* farinaceous; floury
farinhoso (farinhento) (enfarinhado) *a* floury
farinhudo *a* (of fruit &c pulp) farinaceous; floury
farofa *nf* olive oil/butter-cooked cassava; icing-sugar
farófia *nf* meringue; cream-puff; (of confectionery) egg/milk sweet
farra *nf* freshwater fish: lavaret
fárreo *a* wheat
farro *nm* wheat-cake; barley-water
fartar *vt* to satiate; to saturate
farte (farto) (fartalejo) *nm* almond cake
farto *nm* small pastry; almond cake
fartum *nm* rancid smell
fataça *nf* sea fish: striped-mullet
fatacaz *nm* large slice/piece
fataniscas (pataniscas) *nfpl* small deep-fried cod pieces
fateiro *nm* tripe-seller
fatia *nf* slice; piece; cutlet; **~s de maçã frita** apple-fritters; **~-de-parida (fatia-dourada)** fritter

fatiar *vt* to slice; to cut into rashers
fatura *nf* (of restaurant) bill; voucher
faturar *vt* to invoice
fava *nf* broad-bean
fava-da-índia *nf* (of flavouring) tanka-bean
favo *nm* honeycomb; (of confectionery) sweet
fazenda *nf* farm; (of coffee) plantation
fazer *vt* to make; to do; to cook; to prepare; to bake
febra *nf* (of meat) fatless steak; fibre; **~s** pork steaks
fécula *nf* flour; sediment; lees
feculência *nf* sediment; lees
fedegosa *nf* (of plant) stinking goosefoot
feijão *nm* bean; **~-bravo (~-da-praia)** bay-bean; **~ comum (~-de-espanha) (~-roxo)** kidney bean; **~-fava** broad-bean; **~-fradinho (~-frade)** cowpea, adzuki bean; **~-de-lima** lima bean; butter-bean [USA]; **~-manteiga** butter-bean; **~-preto** black-bean; **~-soja** soya-bean; **~ verde** green bean
feijoada *nf* meat/black bean/ dried pork/beef dish
feijoca *nf* large french-bean
feila *nf* fine flour
feitoria *nf* wine-making
felô *nm* [Braz] sugar-plum
fêmea *nf* female
fender *vt* to cleave
feno-grego *nm* fenugreek
fermentação *nf* fermentation; leavening
fermentar (fintar) *vt* ferment; to leaven
fermento *nm* yeast; **~ em pó** baking-powder
ferragem *nf* cutlery
férreo *a* iron
ferro fundido *nm* cast-iron
fervendo *a* boiling
ferventar *vt* to parboil
fervente *a* boiling
ferver *vt* to cook; to boil; **pouco ~ (quente)** (of egg) soft-boiled
fervilhar *vt* to simmer
fervura *nf* boil; boiling; simmer
festa *nf* festival; holiday; feast; **dia de ~** feast-day
festejo *nf* feast
festim *nm* feast; banquet; party
festival *nm* festival
festividade *nf* feast; festival
festo *nm* [Braz] feast; festivity
feverero *nm* February
fiambre *nm* cured cold meat; cold ham; [Braz] packed meal
fibra *nf* fibre
fidalgo (mandubé) (palmito) *nm* freshwater catfish
fidéus *nmpl* vermicelli
fígado *nm* liver
figo *nm* fig
figueira *nf* fig; **~-de-bengala** banyan
filão *nm* loaf

filé *nm* (of meat/fish) fillet; tenderloin; **~ alho e óleo** oil/garlic fillet steak; **bife de ~ mignon** sirloin steak; **~ à parmegiana** mozzarella/tomato/(ham)-covered milanesa fillet steak

filete *nm* (of meat/fish) fillet

filha-de-senhor-de-engenho *nf* [Braz] sugar-cane brandy

filhó *nm* pancake; fritter; tortilla; wafer

filhote (piraíba) *nm* [Braz] Amazon catfish; piraiba

filoxera *nf* phylloxera; vine-pest

filtrar *vt* to filter

filtreiro *nm* filter; percolator; strainer; colander

filtro *nm* filter; percolator; strainer; colander; (of cigarette) filter-tip

fim *nm* end; **~ de semana** week-end

fintar *vt* to leaven; to ferment

fio *nm* (of beans &c) string; **~ de tripa** gut

fio dental *nm* dental floss

firme *a* (of price) fixed

firmeza *nf* firmness

fiúzo *nm* sea fish: smooth dogfish

flã *nf* flan

flamar (flambar) (flamejar) *vt* to flame; to set alight

flamejado *a* flambéed

flamengo *a* (of cheese) dutch

flamiche *nm* leek tart

flanco *nm* (of animal) side

flandres *nm* tin can

flauta *nf* (of champagne glass) flute

floco *nm* flake; (of chocolate) chip

flor *nm* flower; blossom; **~ de farinha** flour; **~ de noz-moscada** nutmeg; mace

florada *nf* (of confectionery) flower-shaped sweet; orange-blossom sweet

florentino *a* florentine; **ovos à ~a** eggs florentine

floresta negra *nf* black forest gateau

fluido *nm* fluid

fofo *a* spongy; fluffy; soufflé

fogaça *nf* large cake/loaf

fogão *nm* cooker; kitchen-range

fogareiro *nm* small cooker

fogo *nm* fire; (of cigarette) light; **alarme de ~** fire alarm; **~ brando** (of cooking temperature) gentle heat

fogo-apagou *nm* scaled dove

folar *nm* Easter pudding

folha *nf* leaf; **~-dourada** star-apple; **~ de louro** bay leaf

folhada *nf* puff-pastry

folhado *a* flaky; *nm* puff-pastry; wafer

folhelho *nm* pod; shell; husk; hull

fome *nf* hunger

fomo *nm* [Braz] (of pan/pot) cassava-root roaster

fondant *nm* (of confectionery) fondant

fontanário *nm* public drinking fountain
fonte *nf* fountain
foqueteiro-galego cobia (cabio) *nm* black bonito
fora *a* (of table) outside
forata *nf* olive press
forfalha *nf* (of bread) crumb
forma *nf* shape; (of jelly &c) mould; baking-tin; (of cheese) press
formar *vt* to shape; to mould
fórmica *nf* Formica®
forminha *nf* small biscuit shape-cutter; wafer
fornada *nf* oven-ful; roasting
fornecedor *nm* purveyor; supplier; caterer
fornimento *nm* provisions
fornir *vt* to supply; *vi* to cater
forno *nm* oven
forrar *vt* to cover; to line
forte *a* (of alcohol) strong; (of food) spicy
fotografia *nf* photography; photograph; **tirar uma ~** to take a photo
foundue *nm* fondue; **~ de queijo** cheese fondue
frachão *nm* sea fish: sand-eel
fradinho *nm* french/dwarf bean; locust lobster
fragária *nf* wild strawberry
framboesa *nf* raspberry
francês *a* French
franco *a* (of alcohol &c) duty-free
franga *nf* pullet, chicken
frangainha (frangainho *nm)* **(franguinho** *nm)* **(franganito** *nm) nf* chicken
frangalhote *nm* cockerel
frangão *nm* young cock; cockerel; **~-do-mar** sea fish: bib (cod variety)
frangelha *nf* cheese-press
frangipana *nf* frangipane; almond cream/paste
frango *nm* chicken; young cockerel; [Braz] roasted corn-cob; sea fish: sharp-nosed shark; **~ a passarinho** deep-fried chicken pieces
frangolho *nm* wheat-meal porridge
frangote *nm* chicken
franguear *vi* to eat roasted corn
franguinho *nm* small chicken
frappé *a* (of drink) frappé; iced
frasca *nf* kitchen utensils; crockery; china; provisions
frascagem *nf* kitchen utensils; bottles
frascaria *nf* bottles
frasco *nm* bottle
frasqueira *nf* (of wine) cellar; wine-rack; cellaret
frasquinho *nm* small flask
frege-moscas *nm(pl)* low-quality eatery
fregereba *nf* sea fish: tripletail
fregona *nf* kitchen-maid
freguês *nm* customer
freira *nf* sea fish: pomfret; [Braz] popcorn

freirinha *nf* box crab
fresco *a* fresh; new; wholesome; un-preserved; fresco
fressura *nf* (of offal) pluck; viscera; heart/liver/lungs
fressureiro *nm* offal seller
fricandó *nm* fricandeau
fricassé *nm* fricassee
frigideira *nf* frying-pan; pan; fry-up
frigir *vt* to fry; to roast
frigorífero (frigorífico) *nm* fridge; freezer; ice-box; (of room) cold-store
frigorificar *vt* (of food) to freeze; to chill
frigorífico *nm* freezer
frio *a* cold; frozen; chilled; cooled
fritada *nf* fried food; roasted food; fritter; poached eggs
fritadeira *nf* deep-fryer
fritalhada (fritangada) *nf* (of meat/fish) badly-cooked roast
fritar *vt* to fry; to bake; to roast
frito *nm* batter; fritter; fried food; *a* fried; deep-fried/battered
fritura *nf* fried food; fritter
frouva *nf* rook
frugalidade *nf* (of diet) frugality
fruita (fruito) *nf(m)* fruit
frumento *nm* cereals; top-quality wheat
fruta *nf* fruit; **~-de-conde** (of fruit) custard-apple, sweetsop; **~-de-condessa** (of fruit) biriba; **~s cristalizadas** crystallized fruit; **~ flambada** fruit flambé; **~-pão** breadfruit; **~s secas** dried fruit; **~s do tempo** fruit of the season; **~s temporãs** early fruit
frutado *a* (of wine) fruity
fruteira *nf* fruit-bowl; fruit-tree
fruteiro *nm* fruit-bowl; fruiterer
frutescência *nf* fruit season
frutilha *nf* [Braz] strawberry
fruto *nm* fruit; berry
frutose *nf* fructose, fruit sugar
frutuoso *a* fruity
fubá *nm* [Braz] maize/rice flour; **~ mimoso** corn starch
fumada *nf* tobacco-smoke
fumado *a* smoked
fumador *nm* smoker
fumante *nm/f* smoker
fumar *vt* (of ham &c) to cure/smoke; (of tobacco) to smoke
fumeira *nf* [Braz] tobacco-pouch
fumet *nm* fumet; fish/meat stock
fumo *nm* smoke; vapour (of wine) nose
fumoso *a* smoky
funcho *nm* fennel; **~-bravo** dill; **~-marinho** samphire; sea fennel
fundagem *nf* sediment; lees; dregs
fundir *vt* to melt; to dissolve
fundo *nm* bottom; base; concentrated base

ingredients; *a* deep; **prato ~** soup-plate
fungão *nm* fungus; mushroom
funil *nm* funnel
fura-festa *nm* (of party) gate-crasher
fúsaro *nm* safflower
futrica *nf* corner-shop; stall; tavern

G

gabião *nm* large basket
gadanha *nf* ladle
gadão *nm* [Braz] good-class cattle
gadaria *nf* [Braz] cattle
gademar *nm* [Braz] (of cattle) zebu-caracu cross
gado *nm* cattle; sea fish: cod; [Braz] freshwater turtle
gaiado *nm* sea fish: skipjack, bonito, tuna
gaivota *nf* (of eggs) gull; **~-preta** teru-tero; plover variety
gajeru (gajiru) *nm* coco plum
galactose *nm* lactose
galantina *nf* galantine; cold meat in aspic
galeota *nf* sea fish: sand-eel
galeto *nm* [Braz] spring chicken; roast spring chicken
galha *nf* (of fish) first dorsal fin
galhateiro *nm* cruet-stand; caster
galheta *nf* cruet; caster
galhudo *nm* sea fish: dogfish
galinha *nf* chicken; hen; **~-anã** sand-grouse; **~-arrepiada** [Braz] (of bird) anguria; **~-brava** black grouse; **~-da-guiné (~-d'angola) (~-da-india)** guinea fowl
galinheiro *nm* poulterer
galinhola *nf* snipe
galiré *nf* [Braz] dwarf hen
galispo *nm* little cock
galo *nm* cock; **~ garnisé** bantam; **~ do mar** sea fish: John Dory; **salgar o ~** to have day's first alcoholic drink; **~ silvestre** grouse; blackcock
galucha *nf* sea fish: bonga
gama *nm* doe
gamba *nf* prawn; shrimp
gamboa *nf* sweet quince variety
gamela *nf* porringer; wood bowl; tray
gamo *nm* (of deer) fallow deer
gana *nf* hunger; appetite
ganga *nf* hazel-hen; sand-grouse
ganso *nm* goose; gander; **~-patola** solan goose; **~ silvestre** brent-goose
gansinho *nm* gosling
garabebel *nm* sea fish: round pompano
garajau *nm* [Braz] (of carrying) crockery basket
garam masala *nf* mixed hot spices
garapa *nf* [Braz] lemon/sugar-cane drink
garção (garçom) *nm* waiter; **~-**

chefe head-waiter
garçonete *nf* waitress; barmaid; stewardess
garfo *nm* fork; ~ **de trinchar** carving fork
gargalaçar *vi* to drink from bottle
gargaleira *nf* (of barrel) peg, plug; peg; spigot; bung
gargalo *nm* (of bottle/jug &c) neck
garganta *nf* throat
garo *nm* lobster; brined/sunned/ ungutted-fish
garoupa (~ preta) *nf* sea fish: grouper; **~-bexiga** sea fish: rock-hind; **~-rajada** sea fish: hamlet fish; **~-são-tomé** sea fish: red grouper
garra *nf* (of chicken &c) claw
garrafa *nf* bottle; bottleful; flask; flaskful; carafe; ~ **bojuda** stoppered bottle, flacon; ~ **térmica** vacuum-flask; ~ **de vidro crystal** decanter
garrafada *nf* bottleful
garrafal *a* bottle-shaped
garrafão *nm* (of bottle) demijohn
garrafaria *nf* (of wine) cellar; bottle-rack
garrafeira *nf* wine-cellar; cellaret
garraio *nm* bullock
garrota *nf* [Braz] yearling; heifer
garupa *nf* haunch
gás *nm* gas; ~ **carbônico** carbon dioxide; **como** ~ *a* gassy
gasolina *nf* petrol
gasosa *nf* soda water; fizz; fizzy lemonade
gasoso *a* gassy
gaspacho *nm* gaspacho; cold spiced vegetable soup
gastrologia *nf* gastrology
gastronomia *nf* gastronomy
gastronômico *a* gastronomic; epicurean
gastronômo *nf* gourmet; gastronome; epicure
gastrópode *nm* gastropod
gata *nf* spotted cat shark; dogfish
gaveta *nf* (of kitchen) drawer
gaze *nm* gauze
gazela *nf* gazelle
gebo *nm* (of cattle) zebu
gelada *nf* [Braz] fruit juice; sherbet
geladeira *nf* [Braz] fridge; freezer; ice-box
gelado *nm* ice-cream; *a* iced; (of drink) frappé
gelador *a* freezing
gelar *vt* to freeze; to chill
gelatina *nf* gelatine; jelly
gelatinoso *a* gelatinous
geléia *nf* fruit-jelly; marmalade; ~ **de carne** aspic; ~ **de frutas** jam; ~ **de laranjas** marmalade; ~ **de mocotó** calf's foot jelly; gelatine
geleira *nf* freezer
geleiro *nm* ice-seller

gelha *nf* withered fruit
gélido *a* frozen
gelo *nm* ice; **com ~** with ice; **~-seco** dry ice
gema *nf* (of egg) yolk
gemada *nf* egg-nog
gemar *vt* to egg-yolk
genebra *nf* gin
genebrada *nf* gin-fizz
gêneros *nmpl* goods; **~ alimentícios** groceries; foodstuff
generoso *a* (of wine) strong; full-bodied
gengibirra *nf* [Braz] ginger-beer; ginger-ale
gengibre *nm* ginger; **~-amargo** (of spice) wild ginger; **bolo de ~** gingerbread; **vinho de ~** ginger-wine
geola *nf* throat; **~-de-pato** vermicelli
gergelim *nm* sesame seeds; sesame cake
gergilada *nf* sesame biscuits (cookies)
gertrudes *nf* stone parsley
giga *nf* flat basket
gigante *nf* sunflower
gigantil *a* (of maize) giant
gigo *nm* wicker basket; hamper
gigô (gigote) *nm* gigot; dish of minced-meat
gim *nm* gin; **~ com soda e limão** gin-fizz; **~ com tônica** gin and tonic
ginja *nf* morello cherry; morello drink
ginjeira-da-jamaica *nf* suriname cherry
ginjinha *nf* morello-ed brandy
ginsém *nm* ginseng
girassol *nm* sunflower; **~-de-batatas** jerusalem artichoke
glacê *nm* glacé; sugared; icing sugar-coated
glacear *vt* to glaze
glaiadina *nf* wine-clarifier
gleucômetro (glicômetro) *nm* glucometer; sugar-level tester
glicose *nf* glucose; dextrose; corn-syrup; grape-sugar
globicéfalo *nm* blackfish
glóbulo *nm* globule
glute (glúten) *nm* gluten
gnu *nm* gnu
gobião *nm* freswater fish: gudgeon
goiaba *nf* guava
goiabada *nf* guava jam
goiamu *nm* crab
gola *nf* gullet
golada (gole *nm)* *nf* sip; gulp
golfinho *nm* sea fish: porpoise; cowfish; **~-branco** beluga
golinho *nm* (of drink) tot; touch; dram; spot
golpe *nm* (of drink) sip; draught
golpeão *nm* (of drink) long draught
goma de mascar (chicle *nm)* *nf* chewing-gum
gomo *nm* (of orange &c) segment; (of garlic) clove; (of

bamboo) shoot

gonguinha *nf* [Braz] cassava/ sugar-cane drink

gonguito *nm* [Braz] sea fish: small catfish

gorar-se *vi* (of eggs) to addle

goraz *nm* (of fish) bream

gordinho *nm* [Braz] harvest fish

gordo *nm* fat; lard; suet; tallow; **leite ~** whole-milk

gordura *nf* fat; shortening; **~ de leite** cream, clarified butter; **~ poliinsaturada** poly-unsaturated fat; **~ de porco** lard; **~ saturada** saturated fat; **sem ~** fat-free

gorduroso *a* (of food) fatty

gorete *nm* [Braz] sea fish: weakfish

gorgoleta *nf* earthenware jug

gorgonzola *nm* (of cheese) gorgonzola

gorjeta *nf* (of gratuity) tip; **dar ~** to tip

gornope *nm* [Braz] sip; draught; dram

goro *a* (of egg) addled

goroba *nf* [Braz] badly cooked meal

gostar *vt* to taste; to sample; to try; to enjoy; to like

gostável *a* tasty; savoury; appetizing

gosto *nm* taste; savour; flavour; *a* **~** (of salt &c) to taste; **~ de rolha** (of turned wine) corked; **tira-~** snack; savoury

gostos-da-vida *nm* plum variety

gostoso *a* tasty; appetizing; delicious; flavoursome

gostosura *nf* enjoyment

gota *nf* drop

gotado *a* (of drops) sprinkled

gotejamento *nm* trickle

gotejar *vt* to drizzle; to trickle

gotinha *nf* small drop, wee drop

grã-besta *nf* elk

Grã-Bretanha *nf* Great Britain

graças *nfpl* (of prayer) grace; **dar as ~** to say grace

grainha *nf* (of fruit) stone; pip

grajau *nm* [Braz] crockery basket

grajéia *nf* (of confectionery) fondant; sweet

gral *nm* mortar

gralha-calva *nf* rook

grama *nf* gram, gramme

grande *nm* large; heavy; plentiful

granita (granito *nm) nf* grape-stone

granja *nf* farm; **~ de avicultura** poultry farm; **~ leiteira** dairy farm

granjeador *nm* farmer

grânulo *nm* grain

grão *nm* grain; cereal; **~-de-bico** chick-pea; **~ de café** coffee-bean; **~ de cevada** barley

grapiapunha *nf* [Braz] squash

graspa *nf* (of wine dregs)

brandy
gratinado *a* au gratin
grátis (gratuito) *a* (of charge) free
grau *nm* (of measurement) degree; unit; grade; **~ centígrado** centigrade
graúlho *nm* grape-stone
gravanço *nm* chick-pea; food, meal
gravata *nf* (of shirt) tie; **~-borboleta** [Braz] bow tie
grave *nm* (of wine) Graves
graviola-do-norte *nf* [Braz] soursop
grelha *nf* grill; barbecue; toaster
grelhado *a* grilled; roasted
grelhar *vt* to fry; to grill; to barbecue; to broil
grifa *nf* claw
grogue *nm* (of drink) grog
grolado *nm* [Braz] (of confectionery) sweet of unpeeled fruit
gronho *nm* pear variety
grosa *nf* (of quantity) gross, twelve-dozen
groselha *nf* currant; gooseberry; **~-preta** blackcurrant
groselheira *nf* (of bush) red currant; **~-branca** white currant; **~-espinhosa** gooseberry; **~-da-índia** star gooseberry; **~-preta** blackcurrant
grossista *nm* wholesaler; *a* wholesale
grossure *nf* thickness; (of animal) fat
grugutuba *nm* bean variety
grulho *nm* corn cob
grunha *nf* pear variety
guacamole *nm* guacamole
guaibira *nf* [Braz] sea fish: leather jack
guajuba *nm* [Braz] sea fish: yellow-tailed snapper
gualá-das-pedras *nm* [Braz] mud crab
gualaba *nf* guava
guanaco *nm* guanaco
guando (guandu) *nm* pigeon pea
guaraná *nm* [Braz] guarana; very strongly caffeinated beverage
guarda *nm/f* policeman/woman; **~-bagagem** *nm* left-luggage; **~-caça** game-keeper; **~-chuva** umbrella; **~-comida** larder; **~-costas** coastguard; **~-fogo** fire-guard; **~-louça** cupboard; side-board; buffet; **~-portão** doorman; **~-roupa** cloakroom; **~-sol** sunshade; parasol; umbrella; Malabar almond
guardadora *nf* cloakroom attendant
guardanapo *nm* napkin, serviette
guarnição *nf* garnish
guelra *nf* (of fish) gill
guia *nf* guide-book; handbook
guisado (guizado) *nm* stew; ragout; [Braz] mince-meat; **~**

de lagostim crayfish bisque; **~ à moda chinesa** chop-suey; *a* stewed
guisar *vt* to stew; to cook; to season
gula *nf* good eating
gulodice *nf* (of confectionery) sweet; titbit; delicacy
gulosar *vt* to nibble
guloseima (gulosice) *nf* (of confectionery) sweet; titbit; delicacy; **~s** delicatessen
gunjiero *nm* Indian licorice
gurutuba *nf* bean variety

H

halabote (alabote) *nm* sea fish: halibut
haliote *nm* mollusc: abalone
hamamélia (hamamélide) (hamamélis) *nf* witch hazel
hambúrguer *nm* hamburger
havana (havano) *nm* (of cigar) havana
haver *vt* to have; **não há de que** (of thanks) don't mention it!
herbanário *nm* herbalist's
herbático (herbóreo) *a* herbal
hiapuá *nm* [Braz] wild cassava
híbrido *nm* hybrid
hidra *nf* dogfish
hidratos de carbono *nmpl* carbobydrates
hidromel *nm* mead
hipoglosso *nm* sea fish: halibut
hissopo *nm* hyssop
hoje *adv* today
holandês *nm* hollandaise
holotúria *nf* sea cucumber, sea slug
hora *nf* hour; time; **~ de [ ]** (of lunch &c) [ ]-time; **~ de fechamento** closing time
horário *nm* schedule; time-table
hordeína *nf* (of protein) hordein
horta *nf* kitchen garden; vegetable garden
hortaliça *nf* vegetables; greens
hortelã *nf* mint; **bala de ~** (of confectionery) peppermint drops; **~-do-campo** wild basil; **essência de ~** extract of peppermint; **óleo de ~** peppermint oil; **~-pimenta** *nf* peppermint
hortulana *nf* ortolan; bunting
hóspede *nm* (of restaurant) guest; customer

I

iabá *nm* [Braz] salted meat
Ibéria *nf* Iberia; Spain and Portugal
icó (icozeiro [Braz]**)** *nm* caper
ictiocola *nf* isinglass
iguano *nm* iguana
iguaria *nf* dish; food; fare; delicacy; custard
imaturidade *nf* unripeness
imaturo *a* unripe
imbu *nm* (of fruit) mombin
imbuzada *nf* (of confectionery)

mombin fruit sweet
imperador *nm* sea fish: red bream
implemento *nm* implement
importação *nf* (of food &c) import
importar *vt* (of food &c) to import
imposto *nm* (of tax) duty; **isento de ~** duty-free, tax-free
impotável *a* impotable, not fit to drink
imprensa *nf* (of cider &c) press
inajá *nm* (of tree) inaja palm
incapacidade *nf* disability
incender *vt* (of flame) to light
incisão *nm* (of meat &c) incision
incluído *a* included
incluir *vt* to include; to add; to mix-in
inclusivo *a* inclusive
incluso *a* included
incomível *a* uneatable
incontaminado *a* unadulterated; pure
incorporar *vt* to incorporate; to add; to mix-in
indaiá *nm* pindova palm
indigerível (indigesto) *a* indigestible
inédia *nf* (of food) abstinence
infusa *nf* earthenware pot
infusão *nf* infusion; essence; extract
ingerir *vt* to swallow
Inglaterra *nf* England; Great Britain
inglês *a* english; **à ~sa** (of cooked vegetables) butter sautéed
inglúvio *nm* (of bird) crop, craw
ingrediente *nm* ingredient
ingresso *nm* entrance
inhame *nm* sweet potato, yam
inoxidável *a* (of steel) stainless
insípido *a* insipid; flavourless; tasteless
insossar *vt* to prepare without salt/seasoning
insosso *a* saltless; unseasoned; tasteless
instruçãoes de manejo *nfpl* operating instructions
insulina *nf* (of diabetes) insulin
insulso *a* saltless; tasteless
inteiro *a* whole; entire
interdito *a* (of entry &c) forbidden, prohibited
interior *nm* interior; intestines
intestino *nm* intestines
inundar *vt* (of liquid) cover-with
inválido *a* (of person) disabled
invernadouro *nm* greenhouse; hothouse
inverno *nm* winter
iogurte *nm* yoghourt
iritinga *nf* sea fish: catfish
irlandês *a* Irish
iró *nf* eel
isabel *nf* vine variety
iscas *nfpl* liver
isqueiro *nm* (of cigarettes &c)

lighter
itacurua *nf* [Braz] (of cooking) three-rock trivet
ituí *nm* freshwater fish: grey catfish

J

jaaraboá *nm* kidney bean
jabá *nm* [Braz] jerked beef; dried meat
jabuti *nm* land turtle
jabuticaba *nf* [Braz] jaboticaba fruit
jaca *nf* jackfruit
jacundá *nm* [Braz] freshwater scale fish: jacunda
jágara (jagra) *nf* dark-brown sugar
jalapa *nf* sour wine
jamanta *nf* sea fish: manta ray
jambé *nm* [Braz] amaranth dish
jambo *nm* jambo
janeiro *nm* January
janela *nf* window; **~ de serviço** serving-hatch
janota *nf* quality control mark
janta *nf* dinner
jantar *nm* dinner; **~ dançante** dinner-dance; **hora de ~** dinner-time; **mesa de ~** dining table; **sala de ~** dining-room; *vi/vt;* to dine; to have to dinner; **~ fora** to dine out
jantarão *nm* feast; banquet
japa *nf* [Braz] (of gratuity) tip
japecanga *nf* sarsaparilla
jardim *nm* garden
jardineira *nf* fresh vegetable garnish
jarro (jarra *nf)* *nm* jug; jar
jatuarana *nm* [Braz] freshwater fish: jatuarana
jaú *nm* freshwater fish: Amazonian giant catfish
javali (javardo) (javalina *nf)* *nm* wild boar
jejuar *vi* to fast; to abstain
jejum *nm* fasting; abstinence
jenipapada *nf* (of confectionery/dessert) genipap
jenipapo *nm* (of fruit) genipap
jequiá *nf* basket
jerepoca (jurupoca) (braço-de-moça) (liro) *nf* freshwater catfish
jerimu (jerimum) *nm* [Braz] pumpkin; squash
jeropiga *nf* brandy/sugar/fruit-juice drink; plonk
jetica *nf* [Braz] sweet potato
jevura *nf* [Braz] Feb/Mar-planted beans
jinjibirra *nf* ginger-beer
jiquitaia *nf* [Braz] pepper sauce; hot sauce; pepper powder
jiritana *nf* bean variety
jovem (jovens *pl)* *a* (of wine) young
juá (jujuba [Braz]) *nm* jujube
judeu *nm* dish of beans; sea fish: frigate tuna
julepo *nm* (of drink) julep
julho *nm* July

juliana *a* finely sliced-vegetabled
jumento *nm* donkey
junho *nm* June
junípero *nm* juniper
juntar *vt* to mix in; to fold in
jupará *nm* [Braz] kinkajou
juquiraí *nm* [Braz] salt/pepper-seasoning
jureminha *nf* mimosa
juriti *nf* [Braz] dove
jurubita *nf* sugar-cane brandy
jurupensém (bico-de-pato) *nm* [Braz] freshwater fish: duck-bill
jurupoca (jerepoca) (braço-de-moça) (liro) *nf* freshwater catfish

K

kebab *nm* kebab
ketchup *nm* ketchup
kg (quilograma) (quilo) *abbr* kilogram
kirsch *nm* kirsch; cherry brandy
kosher *a* kosher
kümmel *nm* kümmel, caraway/cumin liqueur

L

labro *nm* sea fish: bass
lactase *nf* lactase
lácteo (láteo) (lactescente) (latescente) *a* milky
lactescência *nf* milkiness
láctico *a* lactic; **ácido ~** lactic acid
lactose *nf* lactose, milk sugar
lado *nm* side
ladrilho *nm* block of quince marmalade
lagar *nm* (of wine/olive/fruit) press
lagariça *nf* small press
lagarto *nm* (of beef cut) silverside; **~-do-mar** sea fish: lizard fish
lagênula *nf* small flask
lagópode *nm* ptarmigan
lagosta *nf* crawfish; lobster; **~-comum** spiny lobster; **~-gafanhoto** mantis shrimp
lagostim (lagostins *pl)* *nm* king prawn; crayfish; Norway lobster; **~ do rio** crayfish; **guis(z)ado de ~** crayfish bisque
lalbeque *nm* sea fish: rockling
lambaio *nm* [Braz] mop; (of person) scullion
lambança *nf* (of object) eatable
lambão *a* gluttonous
lambareiro *nm* (of person) sweet-tooth
lambari (piaba) *nm* carp freshwater fish: lambari
lambarices *nfpl* (of confectionery) sweets; titbits
lambedine *nm* (of confectionery) sweets; titbits
lambisqueiro *nm* (of person) sweet-tooth; snacker
lambujar *vt* (of confectionery)

to eat/love sweets

lambujeiro *nm* (of confectionery) sweet eater/ lover

lambujem *nf* (of confectionery) sweet

lâmina *nf* (of knife) blade; (of mushrooms &c) slice

laminária *nf* sea cabbage

lãmpada *nm* lamp

lampadário *nm* chandelier; candlestick; candelabrum

lampreia *nf* lamprey; catfish; **~-dos-rios** freshwater lamprey

lanchar *vi* to snack; to breakfast

lanche *nm* elevenses; breakfast

lanchonete *nf* [Braz] snack-bar

langanho *nm* [Braz] cheap meat

languenho *nm* [Braz] cut of cheap meat

lanhar *vt* (of fish) to clean; to gut

lanho *nm* slice of meat; bacon rasher

lapa *nf* limpet; **~-real** scallop

laparão *nm* large limpet

láparo *nm* young rabbit

lápis *nm* pencil

L.B.V. *abbr* late bottled vintage

laranja *nf* orange; **~-amarga (~-azeda) (~-da terra)** bitter orange, Seville orange; **~-da-baía** navel orange; **casca de ~** orange-peel; **~-cravo** [Braz] tangerine, mandarin orange; **espremedor de ~s** orange-squeezer; **~-mimosa** tangerine; mandarin; **~-pêra** small orange variety; **~ de polpa vermelha** blood-orange; **suco de ~s** orange-juice

laranjada *nf* orangeade

laranjeiro *nm* orange-seller

laranjinha *nf* orange-peeled rum

lardear *vt* to lard; (of stuffing) to bacon/pork

lardo *nm* lard; bacon

lasanha *nf* lasagne

lasca *nf* slice; flake

lata *nf* can; tin; (of tea) caddy; (of rubbish) bin

latão *nm* (of milk) churn

latrina *nf* WC

lava-dente *nm* drink

lavabo *nm* (of washing) basin

lavadilha *nf* sea fish: sprat

lavadouro *nm* wash-tub/board

lavadura *nf* dish wash; dish-water

lavagante *nm* european lobster; yabby

lavanda *nf* lavender

lavandeira *nf* plover

lavar *vt* to wash; **~ a louça** to wash-up

lavatório *nm* wash-basin; WC

lavável *a* washable

lebracho *nm* leveret, young hare

lebrada *nf* jugged hare

lebre *nf* hare; **~-marinha** sea

fish: blenny; butterfly fish
lechia *nf* (of fruit) lychee
lecitina *nf* lecithin
legume *nm* legume; vegetable; **~s** greens, vegetables; [Braz] herbs
leguminivoro *a* vegetarian
legumista *nm* vegetable-grower
leitagada *nf* (of pig) litter
leitão *nm* sucking-pig; **~ assado** roasted sucking-pig
leitar *a* milky
leite *nm* milk; **~ de coco** coconut milk; **~ coalhado** sour milk; curd-cheese; **~ condensado** condensed-milk; **creme de ~** heavy cream [USA]; **~ desnatado (~ magro)** skimmed-milk; **~ em pó** powdered milk, dried milk; **~ integral (~ gordo)** full-cream milk, un-homogenized milk
leiteira *nf* milk-jug
leiteiro *nm* milkman; *a* milky
leitelho *nm* buttermilk
leitento *a* milky
leiteria *nf* milk-bar; dairy
leitoa *nf* sucking-pig
leitoada *nf* (of dish) sucking-pig
leitoso *a* milky
lentilha *nf* lentil; **~-d'água** water-lettuce
leocádio *nm* chandelier
lepas *nm* goose barnacle
lepidossirene *nf* freshwater fish: lungfish
leporídeo *nm* hare
leque *nm* scallop
lesma *nf* snail; **~-do-mar** sea cucumber; sea snail
levantar *vt* to stand; (of glasses) to chink; **~ em castelo** (of egg-white) to whip stiff
levante *nm* horsemint
levar *vt* to take; to remove; to contain; to place
leve *a* (of wine) light
levedação *nf* leavening; fermenting
levedar *vt* to leaven; to ferment
lêvedo *nm* yeast; *a* leavened; fermented
levedura *nf* yeast, leaven
leves *nmpl* (of offal) lights
levístico (ligústica *nf)* *nm* lovage
lhama *nm* llama
lia *nm* (of wine &c) dregs, lees, sediment
libar *vt* to drink; to sip
lichi *nf* lychee
licor *nm* liqueur; liquid; post-coffee chaser; **~ açorda de marisco** seafood bread soup; **~ beneditino** Benedictine; **~ de cereja** cherry brandy; **~ digestivo** digestive liqueur
licorista nm/f liqueur-seller
licoroso *a* (of wine) fortified (sweet); liqueury
licuri *nm* [Braz] urucuri palm
ligar *vt* (of cream &c) to bind ingredients
ligeiramente *adv* (of cooking/

heating &c) lightly
ligústica (**levístico** *nm*) *nf* lovage
lima *nf* (of fruit) lime
limada *nf* (of drink) limeade
limão *nm* lemon; **~-galego** citron
limãozinho *nm* small lemon
limar *vt* to add lemon/oil
limeira *nf* lime
limoeiro *nm* lemon tree
limonada *nf* lemonade; **~ gasosa** fizzy lemonade; **soda ~** lemon squash
limonadeiro *nm* lemonade maker/seller
limpa *nf* rum
limpo *a* clean; (of fish &c) skinned; gutted; boned
límulo *nm* king-crab
limusine *nf* limousine
língua *nf* tongue; **~-de-mulata** tongue-fish; **~-de-vaca** ox tongue
linguado *nm* flounder; sole; **~-lixa** tongue-fish
lingue escaldo seco *nm* dried ling, spillanga
lingüeirão *nm* razor-clam
lingüiça *nf* sea fish: red hake; cheap sausage; **~ calabresa** seasoned pork sausage; **~ de fígado** liverwurst; **~ portalegre** garlic/chili/wine pork-sausage
linha *nf* string
liofilizado *a* (of coffee &c) freeze-dried
liquidificador *nm* blender
líquido (**líqüido**) *nm* liquid; drink; *a* liquid, fluid
lírio *nm* sea fish: cutlass-fish; scabbard-fish
liro (**braço-de-moça**) (**jerepoca**) (**jurupoca**) *nm* freshwater catfish
liso *a* (of fish &c) slippery; smooth
lista *nf* menu; **~ de vinhos** wine list; **~ telefônica** telephone directory
listado (**listão**) *nm* skipjack, bonito, tuna
litão *nm* small cured dogfish
litro *nm* litre
lixa *nf* sea fish: dogfish
lobo-do-mar *nm* sea fish: bass
locusta *nf* locust
loja *nf* shop
lojeca *nf* small shop; small pub
lojista *nm/f* shopkeeper
loligideos *nm* squid
lombarda *nf* savoy cabbage
lombinho (**lombilho**) *nm* fillet; tenderloin; smoked pork fillet
lombo *nm* sirloin; tenderloin; fillet; **~ branco de portalegre** slightly spiced salty pork-loin sausage; **~ enguitado de portalegre** slightly spiced chili/garlic pork sausage
longueirão *nm* razor clam
lorcha *nf* sea fish: greenling
lota *nf* fish auctioneer's
lotar *vt* (of wine) to blend

louça *nf* crockery; dishes; chinaware
louçaria *nf* crockery; china shop
louceira (**louceiro** *nm) nf* china cupboard; china seller/maker
louro *nm* bay; **~-amarelo** (of flavouring) onion cordia; **folha de ~** bay leaf
lua *nf* month **~ de-mel** honeymoon
lúcia-lima *nf* lemon verbena
luciano *nm* sea fish: snapper
lúcio *nm* freshwater fish: pike; **~-perca** freshwater fish: pike-perch
lugar *nm* place; seat; **~ de honra** place of honour
lula *nf* squid; **~ fritas** fried squid; **~ recheada** stuffed squid
lume *nm* fire; burner; heat
lumpo *nm* lumpfish
lúpulo *nm* (of beer) hop
lustre *nm* chandelier; candelabrum
lutjanídeos *nm* snapper variety
luxo *nm* luxury
luxuoso *a* luxurious
luz *nf* light
luzerna *nf* alfafa

M

maçã *nf* apple; [Braz] sugar-cane variety; **aguardente de ~** apple-jack; **~-do-amor** whole caramelised apple; **~ para cozinhar** cooking-apple; **~ silvestre (~ azeda)** crab-apple
macaca *nf* [Braz] calfless cow
macaco *nm* monkey
macaia *nf* ([Braz] macaio *nm)* cheap tobacco
maçal *nm* whey
maçangana *nf* (of brandy) sugar-cane
maçanilha *nf* small apple
maçapão *nm* marzipan; (of confectionery) sugar-almond
macarrão *nm* macaroni; noodles; **~ com queijo** macaroni cheese
macarronada *nf* macaroni dish
macarronete *nm* thin macaroni
macaxeira (macaxera) *nf* sweet cassava
macear *vt* to macerate
macedônia *nf* (of vegetable/fruit salad) macédoine
macela *nf* camomile
macerado *nm* macerated
machada *nf* meat-cleaver
machinho *nm* (of horse) fetlock
macho *nm* male animal; eel
machucho (machuchu) (chuchu) *nm* (of fruit) chayote
maciera-da-china *nf* Chinese flowering crab apple
macis *nm* (of spice) mace
maço *nm* (of cigarettes) pack
macuca *nf* wild pear tree

Madeira *nm* (of fortified wine) Madeira
madre *nf* mother of vinegar
maduração *nf* ripening; (of wine) ageing
madurar *vt* to ripen; to mature
madureza *nf* ripeness; maturity
maduro *nm* ripe; mature; (of wine) crusted; [Braz] fermented drink
mãe *nf* mother of vinegar; **~-benta** [Braz] small biscuit
magro *a* thin; weak; (of meat) lean; (of milk) skimmed; (of food) low-fat; **dia ~** day of fasting
magusto *nm* roasted chestnut
maio *nm* May
maionese *nf* mayonnaise
maisena® *nf* corn starch
majorana *nf* marjoram
mal-assada *nf* omelette
mala *nf* suitcase; bag; handbag
malabar *nm* cattle breed
malacozoário *nm* mollusc
malagueta *nf* chili pepper
malaxadeira *nf* butter churn
malcasado (malcassá) *nm* [Braz] coconut/tapioca/milk banana-wrapped pancake
malcozinhado *a* underdone; badly-cooked
malpassado *nm* (of meat &c) rare
malpinguinho *nm* [Braz] tobacco
maltado *a* malted
maltagem *nm* malting
maltar *vt* to malt
malte *nm* malt
maltose *nf* maltose
malvada *nf* [Braz] sugar-cane brandy
malvaísco (malvavisco) *nm* marsh mallow
malvasia *nf* (of fortified wine/ grape variety) malmsey; sweet mellow madeira
mamadeira *nf* (of baby) feeding-bottle
mamão *nm* (of fruit) papaya; young donkey; unweaned calf
mamarreis *nm* [Braz] (of fish) silverside
mampar *vt* [Braz] to eat
maná *nm* manna
manampança *nf* [Braz] cassava confectionery/cake
manauê ([Braz] **manuê)** *nm* corn meal/honey cake
mancheia *nf* handful
manchil *nm* (of butcher) cleaver
mandaçaia ([Braz] **manaçaia)** *nf* honey bee variety
mandarina *nf* mandarin; tangerine
mandi-alumínio (barba-chata) (barbado) (piranambu) *nm* [Braz] freshwater catfish
mandiba *nf* [Braz] cassava variety
mandigüera *nm* [Braz] (of piglet) runt
mandioca *nf* cassava

mandiocaba *nf* [Braz] cassava-ed sweet rice soup; **~-doce** [Braz] sweet cassava
mandubé (palmito) (fidalgo) *nm* freshwater catfish
mandureba *nf* sugar-cane brandy
manema *nm* [Braz] coarse manioc flour
manga *nf* (of fruit) mango
mangalô *nm* [Braz] jack bean
mangangá *nm* scorpion fish
mangarataia *nf* [Braz] ginger
mangonga *nm* sand shark
mangostão *nm* (of fruit) mangosteen
maniçoba *nf* [Braz] cassava-shoot meat/fish dish
manilha *nf* tobacco variety
manipuça *nm* (of fruit) melastoma
maniva (maniveira, manaíba) *nf* manioc, cassava
manja *nf* meal
manjar *vt* to eat; *nm* food; titbit; morsel; pudding; custard; **~-branco** blancmange; (of sweet) milk/coconut/prunes; **~es finos** delicatessen
manjericão *nf* basil
manjerona *nf* marjoram
manjuba (manjuva) ([Braz] **pititinga, pipitinga)** *nf* sea fish: anchovy
manta *nf* sun-dried meat/fish; (of bacon) flitch
manteiga *nf* butter; [Braz] animal/vegetable oil; **~ de amêndoim** peanut butter; **~ derretida** melted butter; **feijão-~** butter-bean; **~ líquida** ghee
manteigaria *nf* dairy
manteigoso *a* buttery
manteigueira *nf* butter-dish
mantel (mantém) *nm* table-cloth
mantimento *nm* provisions
mantopaque *nm* [Braz] freshwater fish; catfish
manzape *nm* [Braz] maize cake; cassava cake; badly baked cake
mão *nf* hand; **~ de gral** pestle; **~-cheia** handful
mão-curta *nm* [Braz] deer variety
mapará *nm* [Braz] catfish
máquina *nf* (of washing-up &c) machine; apparatus; implement; [Braz] car; **~ de picar** mincer; food-processor
mar *nm* sea; **frutos do ~** sea-food
maracauim (chama-maré) *nm* [Braz] crustacean
maracotão *nm* peach variety
maracujá *nm* (of fruit) passionfruit
maragojipe *nm* [Braz] coffee variety
maranho *nm* (of dish) chicken/rice/sheep's pluck; gravy made from giblets
marasca *nf* (of cherry) marasca

marasquino *nm* maraschino; cherry liqueur
marato *nm* fennel
maravilha *nf* pastry; **~-do-sertão** [Braz] herbal tea
marchar *vt* [Braz] to foot the bill
março *nm* March
margarin *nf* margerine
maria-da-serra *nf* freshwater catfish; (of confectionery) jelly/egg-white/sugar/coconut sweet; **~-farinha** crab; **~-mole** (of fish) croaker, drum; **~-da-toca** sea fish: goby
marido *nm* husband
marimbá (marimbau) *nm* [Braz] sea fish: sargo
marinada *nf* marinade
marinar *vt* to marinade
marinas *nf* seaweed
mariquinha *nf* [Braz] kitchen tripod
marisco *nm* shellfish; clam; **sopa de ~** seafood soup
marisqueiro *nm* shellfish seller
marlim *nm* sea fish: marlin
marmelada *nf* quince marmalade
marmeladeiro *nm* quince marmalade seller
marmelo *nm* quince
marmita *nf* marmite
marolo *nm* (of tree) custard-apple
marrã (~o) *nf(m)* weaned young sow/hog; lamb; [Braz] pork
marrar *vi* (of wine) to become cloudy
marreco *nm* [Braz] duck; widgeon; teal; **~ de pequim** Peking duck; sea fish: stumpnose
marruás *nm* [Braz] bull
martel *nm* rural-pub mug
martelo *nm* hammer; sea fish: hammerhead shark; **~ de carne** meat-tenderiser
maruca *nf* sea fish: ling
marufo *nm* (of leguminous tree) fermented sap
marumbé *nm* [Braz] variety of bean
marzipã *nf* marzipan
mascar *vt* to chew; **goma de ~** chewing-gum
mascavado *nm* (of sugar) unrefined; **açúcar ~** brown sugar
mascavinho *nm* brown sugar
mascavo *nm* (of sugar) refining
massa *nf* dough; paste; pasta; ground cassava (manioc); Naples wine; **~s alimentícias** noodles; **~ amanteigada** short-crust pastry; **~ doce** Danish pastry; **~ folhada** puff pastry; **~ podre** short paste [USA]; **~ quebrada** short-crust pastry
massamorda *nf* garlic-ed fried breadcrumbs
massaroco *nm* sour dough
masseira *nf* kneading trough
massinha *nf* soup noodles
massoca *nf* [Braz] cassava

paste
massudo *a* doughy
mastruço (mastruz, mentruz) *nm* bitter-cress
mata-bicho *nm* (of spirits) dram; tot
mata-ratos *nm* cheap wine/ tobacco
matacão *nm* large slice/piece
matadouro *nm* slaughterhouse
matambre *nm* (of beef) rib
matança *nf* [Braz] slaughterhouse
matão *nm* rice variety
matar *vt* to slaughter; (of thirst/ hunger) to assuage; to quench
mate *nm* maté, herbal tea; **~ chimarrão** mate without sugar; **~ de armada curta** very hot maté
matear *vt* to drink maté
mateiro *nm* deer variety
matéria corante *nf* colouring-matter
matetê *nm* thick broth
matricária *nf* chamomile, camomile
matrinxã *nf* freshwater Amazon fish: matrinxã
matrucar *vt* [Braz] (of slaughtered cattle) to cut up
matruco *nm* [Braz] (of slaughtered cattle) hindquarters
matruqueiro *nm* [Braz] butcher
maturação *nm* ripening
maturado *a* ripe; mature; seasoned
maturar *vt* to mature; to ripen
maturidade *nf* maturity; ripeness
mazagrã *nm* iced coffee
mazama *nm* deer variety
mealha *nf* crumb
média *nf* [Braz] white coffee
medida *nf* (of quantity) measure
médio *a* (of steak/temperature &c) medium
mediterrânico *a* Mediterranean
medula óssea *nf* bone-marrow
meia-noite *nf* midnight
meia-pinta *nf* (of measure) cup
meio *nm* half; **~-assado** half-cooked/baked
meio-dia *nm* midday; noon; south
meiru-de-preto *nm* (of plant) custard-apple variety
mel *nm* honey; **~ de engenho** sugar-cane juice; **~ de-pau** tree-bee honey; **~ de toicinho** molasses/bacon syrup; **~ virgem** virgin honey; **lua de ~** honeymoon
melaço *nm* molasses; treacle
meladinha *nf* honey/sugar-cane brandy
melado *nm* [Braz] thick sugar-cane syrup; [Braz] (of dessert) molasses; *a* (of fruit &c) withered
melancia *nf* watermelon; apple

variety
melanciera *nf* watermelon seller
melão *nm* melon; **~-caboclo** [Braz] cassabanana; **~-de-são-caetano** balsam pear
meleiro *nm* honey seller
melhor *a* best
melícia *nf* (of confectionery) cinnamon/almond sweet
melificar *vt* to honey
melindre *nm* asparagus; honey cake
meloso *a* syrupy; sweet; sticky
melro *nm* blackbird
mendubi (mendubim) (menduí) *nm* [Braz] peanut
meninico *nm* lamb-lights dish
mensageiro *nm* bell-boy; button-boy
mensário *a* (of eating) table
menta *nf* mint
mentira-carioca *nf* tapioca biscuit
mera *nf* juniper oil
mercadinho *nm* small market; fruit/vegetable stall
mercado *nm* market; **~ de peixes** fish-market
mercador *nm* merchant
mercearia *nf* grocer's; **~s** groceries
merenda *nf* breakfast; snack; lunch; pack-lunch
merendar *vt* to snack; to breakfast; to lunch
merendeiro *nm* picnic/snack basket; (of person) snacker
merengue (merenque) *nf* meringue
mergulhar *vt* to dunk
merlúcio *nm* sea fish: hake
merma *nf* sea fish: Atlantic little tunny
mero *nm* sea fish: jewfish; grouper; **~ legítimo** sea-perch; **~-prêto** sea fish: black grouper
meru *nm* (of deer) sambar
mês *nm* month
mesa *nm* table; **~ de café** breakfast table; **cama e ~** board and lodging; **~ de cozinha** kitchen table; **~ dobradiça** folding table; **~ elástica** leaf table; **~ de jantar** dining table; **pôr a ~** to lay the table; **~-redonda** table d'hôte; **roupa de ~** table-linen; **sentar-se à ~** to sit down at table; **serviço de ~** dinner service; **servir à ~** to serve/wait at table; **ter boa ~** to keep a good table
messe *nf* crop; harvest
mestiço *nm* [Braz] freshwater fish: sheatfish
mestre-cuca (~ cuco) *nm* cook
metade *nf* half; (of fish) single fillet
metal *nm* metal; **~ais** kitchenware
método *nm* (of recipe) method
mexer *vt* to stir; to shake; (of

eggs) to scramble
mexerica *nf* [Braz] tangerine; mandarin
mexido *nm* (of confectionery) lemon/honey/bread sweet; **ovos ~s** scrambled eggs
mexilhão *nm* mussel
mezenino *nm* mezzanine
micha *nf* bread
mico *nm* [Braz] capuchin monkey
micromicete *nm* yeast
microondas *nm* microwave
miga (migalha) *nf* bread soup
migado *a* minced; sliced; julienne
migalha *nf* crumb; small bit; **~s** leftovers
migalhar (esmigalhar) *vt* to crumble
miger *vt* to crumble
mija-mija *nf* mollusc: cockle
mijuba *nf* yellow manioc
mil-folhas *nm* cream puff pastry
milanesa (à) *nf* (of fillet of steak) floured-egg-covered
milhão *nm* million; maize
milharas *nf* (of fish) hard roe; fig seeds
milhete *nm* maize variety
milho *nm* maize; corn [USA]; **floco de ~** cornflake; **~ verde** cooked sweet corn
milho-zaburro *nm* sorghum
miligrama *nm* milligram; milligramme
mimosa *nf* mandarin; tangerine
minadouro (minadoiro [Braz]) *nm* well, spring, fountain
mineral (minerais *pl) nm* mineral; **água ~** mineral water
mingau de aveia *nm* porridge
míngua *nf* shortage
ministra *nf* (of soup) minestrone
miniuta *nf* [Braz] (of restaurant) instant meal; meal ready in a minute
minuto *nm* (of time) minute
miolada *nf* (of brains) sweetbread
miolo *nm* brain; (of fruit) core; (of bread) soft centre; walnut kernel; pulp of fruit; **~ de amêndoas** ground almonds
mioloso (mioludo) *a* pulpy
mira-olho *nm* peach variety; *a* appetising
miraguaia (piraúna) *nf* sea fish: drumfish
mirandesa *a* (of cattle variety) mirandesa
mirmidão *nm* scullion
mirtilo *nm* blueberry; bilberry; **~ vermelho** cowberry
mirtoso *a* myrtle-containing
missúri *nm* Missouri tobacco
misto *a* mixed
misto-quente *nm* [Braz] toasted ham and cheese sandwich
mistura *nf* mixture; blend; (of whisky) blend
misturada *nf* [Braz] white rum

cocktail
misturar *vt* to mix; to blend; to knead
mitigar *vt* (of thirst) assuage, quench
miudagem *nf* giblets
miudeiro *nm* offal-seller
miudeza *nf* giblets
miúdos *nmpl* giblets
mixórdia *nf* adulterated wine
moagem *nf* (of flour) grinding; milling
moca *nm* (of coffee) mocha; coffee
mochama (muchama) *nf* dried salted tuna strip
mocororó *nm* [Braz] (of rice/ cassava/cashew) soft drink
mocotó *nm* calf's foot
moda *nf* (of cookery) method
moeda *nf* money; coins
moela *nf* gizzard
moer *vt* to mince; to grind; to crush; to press
mofo *nm* mould; mildew; must
moganga *nf* pumpkin variety
môica *nf* [Braz] cassava (manioc) variety
moído *a* crushed; (of coffee) ground; (of meat) minced
moinho *nm* (of coffee &c) grinder; mill
mojica *nf* [Braz] thickened fish stock; thickened stock
molhadela *nf* wetting; soaking; moistening; (of gratuity) tip
molhado *a* wet; moist; **~s** (of oil/wine &c in shop) liquids
molhança (molhanga) *nf* sauce; gravy
molhar *vt* to wet; to dampen; to sprinkle; to dunk; (of gratuity) to tip
molheira *nf* sauce-boat; butter-dish
molho *nm* dressing; sauce; gravy; **~de alcaparra** caper sauce; **~ apimentado** chili sauce; **~ bechamel** bechamel; **~ branco** cream/ white sauce; **~ de chilli** chili sauce; **~ inglês** worcestershire sauce; **~ mostarda** mustard sauce; **~ picante** chutney; **~ de soja** soy sauce; **~ tártaro** tartar sauce; **~ de tomate** tomato sauce; **~ verde** salsa verde; **~ vinagrete** vinaigrette dressing; (of keys) bunch;
molusco *nm* shellfish; mollusc; clam
mombaca *nf* acid fruit
mondego *nm* [Braz] grey mullet
modongo *nm* giblets
mondongueiro *nm* offal-seller
monguba *nf* [Braz] munguba nut
mono *nm* monkey
montês *a* mountain; **cabra ~** chamois; **~ cabrito** ibex
montuava ([Braz] **cachaça)** *nf* white rum
moquear *vt* to grill; (of meat) to dry
moqueca *nf* [Braz] dendê-oiled/

stewed fish/mussels dish
moquém ([Braz] **moqueteiro)** *nm* (of meat/fish) grill
moquenca *nf* garlic-ed/vinegar-ed/peppered beef stew
moranga *nf* grape variety; [Braz] squash variety
morango *nm* strawberry
morangueiro *nm* strawberry seller/plant
morcego-do-mar *nm* sea fish: batfish
morcegueira *nm* [Braz] cabbage tree
morcela (morcilha) *nf* black pudding sausage; **~ de arroz** slightly spiced riced pork sausage; **~ de assar de portalegre** smoked/garlic/chili black pork sausage
mordacidade *nf* (of taste) piquancy
mordaz *a* piquant
morder *vt* [Braz] to have a drink (alcoholic)
mordomo *nm* butler; major-domo
moréia *nm* moray eel
morena *nf* partridge; paca
morgados *nmpl* pastry
morinda *nf* Indian mulberry
moringa (moringue) *nf* water-cooling earthenware jar
morno *a* lukewarm
morsegão *nm* bite; pinch
morsegar *vt* to nibble
mortadela *nf* large Italian sausage
mortificação *nm* (of game/meat) hanging
mosca-das-frutas *nf* fruit-fly
moscadeira *nf* (of tree) nutmeg
moscado *a* aromatic; **noz ~a** nutmeg
moscatel *nm* muscatel; apple/pear/fig variety
mostaço *nm* (of new wine) must
mostarda *nf* mustard
mostardeira *nf* mustard pot/plant
mostardeiro *nm* mustard pot/seller
mosto *nm* (of new wine) must
motorista *nm* motorist; **~ de praça** taxi driver
motoro *nm* (of fish) ray
mouro *a* (of dish) moorish
moxama *nf* dried and salted fish
moxamar *vt* to smoke fish
moxar *vt* to smoke fish
mozarella *nm* (of cheese) mozzarella
muçarete *nm* [Braz] sea snail
muçuã *nm* small turtle
mucubu *nm* haunch of cattle
muçurango *nm* [Braz] freshwater fish: goby
mugem *nf* sea fish: mullet
mujangüê (mujanguê) *nm* [Braz] gulls egg/turtle dish
mulata *nf* potato variety; (of fish) yellow-tailed snapper
mulatinho *nm* green bean variety

mulato-valho *nm* [Braz] salted and dried catfish
mulher *nf* woman; wife
mulso *nm* (of honey) mead
mundéu (mundé) *nf* [Braz] wild hog
mungunzá (munguzá) (mugunzá) *nm* [Braz] coconut/syrup/corn dish
munhata *nf* [Braz] sweet potato
murciana *nf* cabbage variety
murici (muricizeiro) *nm* [Braz] byrsonima fruit
murta (murteira) *nf* myrtle
murtinho *nm* myrtle berry
musa *nf* banana
muscadínea *nf* muscadine grape
musculina *nf* preparation of beef
músculo *nm* muscle; (of beef cut) leg
música ambiental (~ de fundo) *nf* background music
musse (mousse) *nf* mousse; **~ de café** coffee custard mousse; **~ de chocolate** chocolate mousse
musselina *nf* mousseline; creamed hollandaise sauce

N

nabada *nf* dish of turnips
nabo *nm* turnip
naca (nacada) (nacado *nm) nf* chop; piece; slice; portion; (of tobacco) plug
nada *nm* nothing; **de ~!** (of thanks) don't mention it!
nadadeira *nf* (of fish) fin
nádega *nf* rump
naja *nf* spittoon
napar *vt* (of sauce &c) to thickly cover
narceja *nf* game bird: snipe
nariz *nm* nose
nata *nf* cream; **~ azeda** clotted cream; **~ batida** whipped cream; chantilly; **pastéis de ~** egg-custard tarts
natadeira *nf* milk-curdling dish
natado *a* creamy
natal *nm* birthday; Christmas
natural *nm* natural
necessárua *nf* WC
néctar *nm* (of drink) nectar
nectarina *nf* nectarine
negociante *nm/f* (of wine &c) retailer/merchant
negrinho *nm* [Braz] coffee grains
nervo *nm* gristle
nêspera *nf* loquat; medlar
neve *nf* snow
nhamdu *nm* [Braz] (of bird) nandu; rhea
nhoque *nm* gnocchi; dumpling
ninho de salangana *nm* (of soup) bird's-nest
nisa *nm* semi-hard ewe's milk cheese
nogada *nf* (of confectionery/ sauce) nut
nogado *nm* nut-cake; (of

confectionery) nougat
nogueira-pecã *nf* (of nut tree) pecan
noite *nf* evening; **boa-~!** goodnight!
nome *nm* name; **~ de batismo** Christian name, first name; **~ de familia** surname
nouilles *nmpl* noodles
nove *nm* (of number) nine
novembro *nm* November
novidade *nf* harvest
novilha *nm* heifer
novilho *nm* bullock
novo *nm* new; young
noz *nf* nut; walnut; **~ branca** butternut; **~ de caju** cashew nut; **casca de ~** nutshell; **~ de cola** cola nut; **~-moscada** nutmeg
nuca *nf* neck
nucular *a* nut-containing
nugá *nm* nougat
número *nm* number; quantity; amount
nutrição *nf* nutriment; nourishment; nutrition
nutridor (nutriente) *a* nutritious, nourishing
nutrimental *a* nutritious
nutrimento *nm* food, nutriment
nutrivo *a* nutritious, nourishing
nutriz *a* nutritious

O

oanaçu *nm* [Braz] (of palm tree) curuaobarana *nf* [Braz] sea fish: ladyfish
obeba (oveva) *nf* [Braz] sea fish: croaker
obreira *nf* puff pastry
obrigado *excl* thanks!
obtenível *a* available
oceano *nm* ocean; sea
octópode *nm* octopus
odor *nm* aroma; smell; perfume
oficina *nf* (of large house &c) pantry/storeroom/scullery
oito *nm* (of number) eight
olá! *excl* hello!
oleado *nm a* oily
oleideo *a* oily
óleo *nm* oil; **~ de amendoim** peanut oil; **~ de baleia** whale oil; **~ de coco** coconut oil; **~ de milho** cornflour; **~ de oliva** olive oil
oleoso *a* oily; greasy
oleráceo *a* edible
olha *nf* stew; hotchpotch; **~-podrida** spanish stew
olhete (pitangola) *nf* sea fish: yellowtail, amberjack
olho *nm* eye; **~-d'água** *nm* (of water) spring; **~-de-boi** sea fish: amberjack; **~-de-sogra** (of confectionery) prune coconut sweet; **~-de-vidro** [Braz] sea fish: squirrel fish
oliva *nf* olive
omeleta *nf* omelette
omelete *nf* [Braz] omelette; **~ de presunto** ham omelette; **~ de queijo** cheese omelette
onça *nf* ounce; **~ fluida** fluid

ounce
ontem *nm* yesterday
onze *nm* (of number) eleven; **~-horas** sun-flower
ora-pro-nóbis *nm* Barbados gooseberry
orçaneta *nf* (of food colouring) alkanet
orchata *nf* orgeat
orégano *nm* oregano
orégão *nm* sweet majoram
orelha *nf* ear; **~ do mar** scallop; **~-de-curro** rough comfrey; **~-de-judas** (of mushroom) jew's ear
orelhão *nm* public (street) telephone
orgânico *a* organic
origem *nf* (of country/region) origin
original *nm* original
orizicultura *nf* rice-growing
órobo *nm* Sudan cola-nut
ósseo *a* bony
osso *nm* bone; **sem ~s** boneless
ostra *nf* oyster; **~ americana** Virginia oyster; **~-portuguesea** Portuguese oyster
ostreicultura *nf* oyster farming
ouriço *nm* hedgehog; **~-cacheiro** coendou; **~-do-mar (pindá)** sea-urchin, sea hedgehog
outono *nm* autumn
outubro *nm* October
ouvido *nm* ear
ovas *nf* roe
oveiro *nm* egg-cup
ovelha *nf* ewe
ovelhum *a* (of sheep) ovine
oveva (obeba) *nf* [Braz] sea fish: croaker
ovo *nm* egg; **batedor de ~s** egg-beater; egg-whisk; **~ choco (~ podre)** bad egg; **clara do ~** egg-white; **~ cozido** hard-boiled egg; **~ duro** hard-boiled egg; **~ escaldado** poached egg; **~ estrelado** fried egg; **~ fresco** new-laid egg; **gema do ~** egg-yolk; **~s mexidos** scrambled eggs **~s moles** egg paste pastries; **~ de páscoa** Easter egg; **~ pochê (~ quente)** poached egg; **~ quente (~ mole)** soft-boiled egg
oxicoco *nm* cranberry

P

pá *nf* (of meat) shoulder; **~ de lixo** dustpan
paca (pacapacoba) (pacova) (banana) *nf* banana
paçoca *nf* [Braz] meat/cassava dish; **~ doce** (of confectionery) cassava/ peanut/sugar stuffing
paçu *nm* freshwater snapper variety
padaria *nf* bakery
padeiro *nm* baker

padejador *nm* baker
padu *nm* [Braz] (of shrub) coca
pãezinho *nm* bread/potato roll
pagar *vt* to pay; **~ por si** to go dutch; **~ à vista** to pay cash
pagável *a* payable
pagro (pargo) (paguro) *nm* sea fish: porgy; red snapper
paguro *nm* hermit crab
painço *nm* millet
painho de portalegre *nm* lightly smoked spiced chili/ garlic pork sausage
paio *nm* smoked pork sausage
país *nm* country
paladar *nm* taste; flavour; palate; **ao ~** (of salt &c) to taste
palato *nm* palate
paleta *nf* shoulder
palha *nf* (of potatoes/cheese/ drinking) straw; **~ abrantes** egg-yolk pastry
palhete *a* (of wine) claret
palito *nm* toothpick; match; (of fish &c) finger
palma *nf* palm; **óleo de ~** palm-oil
palmatória *nf* prickly pear
palmeta (palometa) *nf* sea fish: bonito
palmito *nm* palm cabbage; **~ (mandubé) (fidalgo)** freshwater catfish
paloco *nm* sea fish: pollack
palombeta (palometa) *nf* [Braz] sea fish: pompano
pamonha *nf* traditional Brazilian corn-husk-wrapped corn paste
pâmpano *nm* sea fish: pompano; **~-manteiga** harvestfish, butterfish
pamparra *a* delicious; tasty
pamplo (pampo) *nm* sea fish: pomfret, pompano, butterfish
panada *nf* panada
panado *a* breaded
panar *vt* to crumb; to bread
panasco *nm* parsnip
pando *a* full; replete
panela *nf* pot; pan; **~ de pressão** pressure cooker
panelada *nf* panful
panelinha *nf* small pan/pot
panificação *nf* breadmaking
panificador *nm* baker
panificadora *nf* [Braz] bakery
pano *nm* dish-cloth; duster
panqueca *nf* pancake
pão *nm* bread; loaf; **~ de açúcar** sugar-loaf; **~ ázimo** unleavened bread; **de batata** potato bread; **~ branco** white bread; **~ caseiro** home-baked/ made bread; **~ de centeio** brown bread; rye bread; **~ na chapa** toast; **~ de forma** sandwich loaf; **fruta-~** breadfruit; **~ de gengibre** (of biscuit) brandy-snap; **~ integral** wholemeal bread; **~-de-ló** sponge-cake; **~ com manteiga** bread and butter; **~ de milho** maize cake; Johnny-cake [USA]; **miolo de**

~ breadcrumb; **pudim de ~** bread pudding; **~ de rala** brown bread; almond-pastry-wrapped white pumpkin-sweet; **~ ralado** bread-crumbs; **~ seco** unbuttered bread; **~ de segunda** brown bread; **~ sírio** pitta bread; **~ torrado** toast

pãozinho *nm* (of bread) roll; **~ francês** french roll

papa de aveia *nf* flummery

papa-defuntos *nm* [Braz] armadillo;

papa-terra *nm* sea fish: king whiting, southern kingfish; [Braz] **~ (curimbatá) (curimatã) (curimatá) (curimba)** freshwater Amazon scale fish

papagaio *nm* sea fish: ladyfish

papala *nf* papaya

papar *vt* to eat

paparicar *vi* (of food) to pick at

paparicos *nm* titbits

papel *nm* paper; paper money; **~ de filtro** filter paper; **~ higiênico** toilet paper; **~ impermeável** grease-proof paper; **~ de seda** tissue paper

papelotes *nmpl* (of cooking) greased paper/foil wrapper

papo-de-anjo *nm* angel-cake; (of confectionery) egg-yolk syrup-ed sweet

par *nm* pair; (of game-birds) brace

pára-sol *nm* parasol; sunshade

paratudo *nm* rattlesnake bean

pardal *nm* sparrow

pargo (pagro) (paguro) *nm* sea fish: snapper, porgy; **~-branco** grunt; **~-legítimo** sea bream

pariri (jurutipiranga) *nf* partridge dove

parmesão *nm* Parmesan

parquímetro *nm* parking-meter

parra *nf* vine leaf

parrilhada *nf* hot spicy seafood dish

partir *vi* to leave; to go

paru *nm* sea fish: butterfly fish

parud-de-dourado (paru-doirado) *nm* [Braz] harvest fish

parva *nf* breakfast

Páscoa *nf* Easter

passa *nf* raisin

passado *a* (of fruit &c) over-ripe; **bem ~** (of steak) well-cooked, well done; medium; au point; **mal ~** rare; under-done

passador *nm* colander; strainer; **~ chinês** piping-bag

passaporte *nm* passport

passar *vt* (of salt &c) to pass

pássara *nf* [Braz] turkey

passarinho *nm* small bird

pássaro *nm* bird

passiflora *nf* passionflower

pasta *nf* paste; dough

pastel *nm* pastry; pie; deep-fried pastry savoury; **~ doce** sweet-filling deep-fried pastry

pastelão *nm* big pie
pastelaria *nf* pastry shop; patisserie
pasteleiro *nm* pastry cook
pasteurizar (pastorizar) *vt* to pasteurise; to sterilise
pastilha *nf* (of confectionery) sweet
pasto *nm* down-market restaurant; food
pastoso *a* doughy
pastrame *nm* pastrami
pata *nf* sea fish: shovelhead shark; **~-roxa** dogfish
pataniscas (fataniscas) *nfpl* (of fish, mushroom &c) battered piece/ball
pataquinha *nf* [Braz] pigeon variety
patê *nm* pâté; **~ de figado** liver pâté
patinho *nm* duckling
pátio *nm* courtyard
pato *nm* duck; **~ almiscarado** musk duck ; **~ bravo (putrião)** (of duck) mallard; **~ com laranja** duck in orange sauce; **~ novo** duckling
patola *nf* (of crab &c) claw
patureba *nm* dried and salted catfish
patuscada *nf* banquet
patusco *nm* feaster
pau-decurtume *nm* locustberry
pauzinhos *nmpl* chopsticks
pavão (pavoa *nf) nm* peacock
pavê *nm* (of confectionery) liqueur-ed sweet
pé *nm* foot; trotter; (of vegetable) stalk; **~-de-moleque** (of confectionery) peanut sweet
pecari *nm* wild pig
pectina *nf* pectin
pedacinho *nm* (of amount) small piece
pedaço *nm* piece; bit; chunk; bite; slice; portion; **~ de sabão** (of soap) bar
pedra *nf* [Braz] draught beer mug
pegar *vt* to stick (to)
peito *nm* (of fowl &c) breast; **~-de-forno** (of dish) lemon-ed turtle
peixão *nm* large fish
peixe *nm* fish; **~ de água doce** freshwater fish; **almôndega de ~** fishball; **~-angulha** sea fish: needlefish; **~-anjo** sea fish: angelfish; **~-aranha** sea fish: greater weever; gurnard; **~ assado** fried fish; **~-bola** sea fish: puffer; **bolo de ~** fish-cake; **~-borboleta** sea fish: butterfly fish; **~-cabra** sea fish: red gurnard; **peixe-cachorro (ueua) (saicanga)** [Braz] freshwater fish: saicanga; **caldo de ~** fish stock; **~-cavalo** sea fish: moonfish; **~ chato** flatfish; **~-cobra** [Braz] snake eel; **~-cravo** sea fish: kingfish, moonfish, sunfish; opah; **~**

defumado smoked fish; **~-elétrico** sea fish: electric eel; **~-espada** sea fish: swordfish; **~-espada preto** sea fish: black scabbardfish; **~ frito** fried fish; **~-galo** [Braz] sea fish: john dory; **~-gato** catfish; **~-lenha** freshwater fish: whip surubim; **~-luna** sea fish: ocean sunfish; **~-macaco** [Braz] blenny; **~ manteiga** butterfish; **~-martelo** sea fish: hammerhead shark; **moqueca de ~** dendê-oiled/stewed fish/mussels dish; **~-morcego** sea fish: batfish; **~-papagaio** parrot fish; **pasta de ~** fish paste; **~-pescador** angler fish; **posta de ~** fish steak; **~-prata-do-Atlântico** silverfish; **pudim de ~** fish balls; **~ rei** silverside, sand smelt; **~ salgado** salt-fish; **~-de-São-Pedro** Saint Peter fish, john dory; **~-serra** sea fish: bonito; sawfish; **terrina de ~** fish pie; **~ vermelho** redfish; **~-voador** sea fish: flying-fish; batfish

peixeiro *nm* fishmonger

peixinho *nm* fry

peixota *nf* sea fish: hake

péla *nf* bark of cork tree

pelar *vt* to skin; to peel

pele *nf* skin; peel; rind; hull; shell; **sem ~** (of fish &c) skinned

película *nf* film; thin skin

peltre *nm* pewter

pema (tarpão) (pirapema) (camurupim) *nf* sea fish: tarpon; silverfish

pena *nf* feather

penca *nf* stalk; stem; (of grapes &c) bunch

peneira *nf* filter; sieve

peneirar *vt* to filter; to sieve

peneiro *nm* large sieve

peniscar *vt* to nibble

penisqueiro *a* nibbling

pensão *nm* boarding house

penteola *nf* escallop, scallop

pepinar *vt* [Braz] to nibble at

pepino *nm* cucumber; **~ em conserva** gherkin

pepitória *nf* chicken giblets

pepônio *nm* pepo; pumpkin

pequeno *a* small; little

pêra *nf* pear

perada *nf* pear conserve; (of drink) perry

perca *nf* sea fish: bass; perch

perceba (percebe *nm)* **(perceve** *nm) nf* acorn barnacle; goose barnacle

percevejo *nm* barnacle

percolador *nm* percolator

perdão! *nm* sorry! excuse me!

perdigão *nm* partridge; tinamou

perdigoto *nm* young partridge

perdiz *nf* partridge; [Braz] tinamou

pereira *nf* pear-tree

perigosa ([Braz] **cachaça)** *nf* white rum

perna *nf* leg
pernil *nm* ham; (of pork) *(usu* roast) leg; joint
peroleira *nf* earthenware olive storage-jar
perrexil *nm* parsley; appetiser
persiana *nf* Persian/Venetian blinds
peru *nm* turkey; **~ assado** roast turkey; **~ recheado** stuffed turkey
perua *nf* turkey hen
peruruca *nf* [Braz] Indian corn variety
pesa-álcool (pesa-licores) *nm* alcoholometer
pesado *a* heavy
pesar *nm* to weigh
pesca *nf* fishing
pescada *nf* sea fish: hake, whiting; croaker; freshwater croaker; **~-carvoeira** sea fish: saithe; **~-polacha** sea fish: pollack, pollock; **~-preta** sea fish: black-fish; sea bass; king george whiting
pescado *nm* fish
pescoço *nm* neck
pessegada *nf* peach preserve
pêssego *nm* peach
petigris *nm* grey squirrel
petiscar *vt* to nibble
petisco *nm* titbit
petromizonte *nm* sea fish/ freshwater fish; lamprey
pevide *nf* (of apple &c) core; pip
pevitada *nf* crushed kernels
pezinho *nm* bread roll
pia *nf* (of kitchen) sink
piaba (lambari) *nm* carp freshwater fish: lambari
piapara (piau) *nm* [Braz] freshwater ray-finned fish
piau (piapara) *nm* [Braz] freshwater ray-finned fish
piavuçu *nm* [Braz] freshwater fish: piavuçu; piau
picadinho *nm* (of meat) minced; (of vegetables) chopped
picado *nm* minced meat; *a* chopped; minced
picante *nm* appetizer; *a* (of chili &c) hot
picar *vt* (of meat) to mince; to chop
picatoste *nm* egg/mutton/ bread-stuffing
pichel *nm* silver/pewter tankard
pichelim *nm* sea fish: blue whiting
pilão *nm* pestle
pilé *nm* rock/granulated sugar
piloto *nm* sea fish: pilot-fish
pilrito *nm* (of berry) haw
pimenta *nf* pepper; (of dish/ ingredient) à la king; **~-d'água** [Braz] water pepper; **~ de caiena** cayenne pepper; **~-de-cheiro** [Braz] cherry pepper; **~-cumari** bird pepper; **~-da-jamaica** allspice; **~ malagueta** ; **~ preta** black pepper; **~-do-reino** black pepper
pimentão *nm* pimento; green

pepper; (of dish/ingredient) à la king; Spanish paprika; **~-comprido (pimpilim)** long pepper; **~-doce** bonnet pepper

pimenteira (~ à mesa) *nf* pepper-pot; **~ moedor** pepper-mill

pimpão *nm* freshwater fish: carp

pimpinela *nf* anise

pinça *nf* tongs; **~ para açúcar** sugar tongs

pindá *nm* sea urchin

pinga *nf* [Braz] rum; white rum; (of alcohol) drink; drop

pingadeira *nf* (of meat) drip-pan

pingado *a* sprinkled; (of coffee) milk-splashed

pingo (pingue) *nm* (of fat) dripping

pinha *nf* [Braz] sweetsop, sugar apple, custard apple; **~-o-penedo (percebe)** *nm* acorn barnacle

pinhão (pinhões *pl)* *nm* pine-nut; piñon

pinheira *nf* (of tree) sweetsop

pintada *nf* Guinea fowl

pintado *nm* sea fish: mackerel; **~ surubim** freshwater fish: stripped catfish

pintainho *nm* young chicken

pintão *nm* small chicken

pintar *vt* to paint; to brush-on

pintinho *nm* young chicken

pipa *nf* barrel

pipeta *nf* pipette

pipi *nm* (of mollusc) pipi

pipo *nm* keg; cask

pipoca *nf* popcorn

piracanjuba *nm* [Braz] freshwater fish: piracanjuba

piracirica *nm* [Braz] sea fish: sand whiting

piracuí *nm* (of dish) dried fish

piraíba (filhote) *nm* [Braz] Amazon catfish

piranambu (mandi-alumínio) (barba-chata) (barbado) *nm* [Braz] freshwater catfish

piranha *nf* [Braz] piranha

pirão *nm* [Braz] cassava paste

pirapema (tarpão) (pema) (camurupim) *nf* sea fish: tarpon; silverfish

pirapitinga (caranha) *nm* [Braz] freshwater fish: black pacu

piraputanga *nf* [Braz] freshwater fish: piraputanga

pirarara *nf* [Braz] freshwater fish: red-tail catfish

pirarucu *nm* [Braz] freshwater fish; pirarucu

piraúna (miraguaia) *nf* sea fish: drumfish

pires *nm* saucer

piri-piri (peri-peri/peli-peli) *nm* (of spice) peri-peri; sauce

pirulito *nm* lollypop

pisa *nf* (of grapes) treading

pisada *nf* grape-treading

pisador *nm* wine-press; (of person) wine-treader

piscina *nf* swimming-pool
pissala (garo *nm)* *nf* brined/sunned/ungutted-fish sauce
pistácio *nm* pistachio
pitada *nf* (of salt/snuff &c) pinch
pitanga *nf* fruit of Surinam cherry
pitangola (olhete) *nf* sea fish: yellowtail, amberjack
pitar *vt* (of tobacco) to smoke
piteira *nf* cigarette-holder
pitéu *nm* titbit; delicacy
pitu *nm* [Braz] large prawn
pixurim *nm* sassafras
pizza *nf* pizza; **~ calabresa** sausage pizza; **~ de frango com catupiri** chicken/Brazilian processed cheese pizza; **~ margherita** mozzarella/tomatoes/basil pizza; **~ mozzarella** plain pizza; **~ portuguesa** ham/onion/egg pizza
pó *nm* powder
poço *nm* (of water) well; **~ artesiano** artesian well
poejo *nm* very fine flour
poia *nf* (of bread) large flat loaf
pojadouro (pojadoiro) *nm* beef-cut topside
polenta *nf* polenta
polha *nf* chicken; pullet
polme *nm* (of consistency) pulp; roux
polpa *nf* pulp; (of fruit &c) flesh
polposo (polpudo) *a* pulpy
polvilhar *vt* to flour; (of ingredient) to dust; to sprinkle
polvilho *nm* cassava (manioc) flour
polvo *nm* octopus
pomátomo *nm* sea fish: bluefish
pomba *nf* pigeon
pombeiro *nm* chicken/pigeon/fish-seller
pombinho *nm* small dove/pigeon
pombo *nm* pigeon
pomelo *nm* grapefruit [USA]
pomo *nm* fruit
ponche *nm* (of drink) punch; **~ de vinho tinto** claret-cup
poncheira *nf* punch-bowl
ponteira *nf* cigarette holder
ponto *nm* point; **ao ~** (of steak) medium; **~ de congelamento** freezing point; **~ de ebulição** boiling point; **~ de fusão** melting point; **~ de táxi** taxi rank
pontual *nf* punctual
poqueca *nf* [Braz] well seasoned fish stew
pôr *vt* (of table) to lay
porão *nm* cellar
poraquê *nm* electric eel
porca *nf* (of pig) sow
porção *nf* (of portion) helping
porcelana *nf* china; porcelain; earthenware; (of herb) green purslane
porcino *a* porcine
porco *nm* pig; pork; sea fish: dogfish; **~ a alentejana** (of

dish) clam/red-peppered diced marinated pork; **~-marinho** pilot whale; **~-montês** wild boar

porongo (porongueiro) *nm* calabash gourd

pororoca *nf* popcorn

pororom *nm* low-quality fruit

porquinho-da-índia (cobaia *nf) nm* guinea-pig

porrada *nf* leek-inclusive stew

porre *nm* (of brandy) swig

porro *nm* leek

porta *nf* door; entrance; gate; **~-bebê** carry-cot; **~-cigarros** cigarette-case; **~ corrediça** sliding door; **de ~s a dentro** indoors; privately; **~ de emergência** emergency door; **~ de frente** entrance; **~ dos fundos** back-door; **~ giratória** revolving door; **~-janela** french window; **~-toalhas** towel rack

portador *nm* porter

porteiro *nm* doorman

porto *nm* (of fortified wine) port

português *nm* Portuguese

pós-perna *nf* (of animal) upper thigh

pospasto *nm* dessert

posta *nf* (of fish &c) slice, cut, chop

postejar *vt* to slice

postergar *vt* to postpone

posto *nm* post; **~ de gasolina** filling station; **~ policial** police station; **~ de pronto-socorro** first aid post; **~ de salvamento** lifeguard; **~ de telefone público** public call-box

postre *nm* dessert

potagem *nf* soup

potável *a* drinkable

pote *nm* jar

potente *a* potent; strong

potério *nm* (of herb) burnet

poti *nm* [Braz] shrimp; prawn

potiúna *nm* [Braz] dark shrimp variety

potra *nf* squid

praça *nf* market-place; square; **carro de ~** taxi

praia *nf* beach

prajá *nm* [Braz] (of confectionery) molasses sweet

pralina *nf* praline

prancheta *nf* knife block

prândio *nm* dinner

prata *nf* silver; silverware; **~ em folhas** silver foil; **bodas de ~** silver wedding

pratada *nf* plate; plateful

pratalhada *nf* (of food) plateful

pratalhaz (pratarraz) *nm* (of food) full plate

prataria *nf* silverware

prateleira *nf* shelf; (of bottles) rack

pratibu *nm* sea fish: mullet

pratinho *nm* small plate

pratiqueira *nf* [Braz] sea fish white mullet

prato *nm* plate; dish; meal; (of

meal) course; helping; **~ cotidiano** regular menu item; **~ do dia** dish of the day; **dois ~s** (of meal) two-courses; **~ especial** side-dish; **~ feito** (of dish) rice/beans/steak/egg/salad; **~ fundo** soup plate; **lavadeira de ~s** (of female) washer-up; **~ de meio** side-dish; entremet; **~ principal** main course; main dish; **~ raso** dinner plate; **~ de resistência** pièce de résistance; **~ secundário** side-dish; entremet; **~ de sobremesa** dessert plate

preçário *nm* price list

preço *nm* price; **~ baixo** small charge; **por bom ~** cheap; **~ elevado** high price; **~ excessivo** overcharge; **~ fixo** fixed price; **~s reduzidos** reduced prices; **~ com tudo incluído** all-inclusive price

precoce *a* unripe

preferência *nf* choice

preferir *vt* to prefer; to select; to choose

pregado *nm* sea fish: turbot

preguari *nm* [Braz] conch

preguiçosa *nf* deck-chair

pregustação *nf* pre-tasting

pregustar *vt* to pre-taste

prejereba *nf* sea fish: triple-tail

prematuro *a* unripe

prenome *nm* Christian name; first name

prensa *nf* press; **~ de vinho** wine-press

prensado *a* squeezed

prensar *vt* to press; to crush; to squeeze

preparação *nf* (of recipe &c) preparation

preparar *vt* to prepare

presente *nm* gift

presigo *nm* (of ham &c) bread-accompaniment

pressão *nf* pressure; **panela de ~** pressure cooker

presunto *nm* ham; smoked ham; gammon; **~ barroso** ham from young pig; **~ cozido** cooked ham

preto *a* black

primavera *nf* spring

primeiro *a* prime; first; **~ andar** first floor; **de ~a** (of meat quality &c) prime; top; first; quality

pristídeos *nm* sea fish: sawfish

privada *nf* WC; toilet; bathroom

proibido *a* prohibited; forbidden

pronto *a* ready; prepared; OK!

propina *nf* gratuity; tip

propinação *nf* drinking the health of; proposal of a toast

propinador *nm* drinker of the health of; proposer of a toast

propinar *vt* to drink the health of; to propose a toast

propriedade *nf* property

proteína *nf* protein

proto *nm* rye-maize bread

prova *nf* taste; savour; sample
provar *vt* to taste; to savour; to sample
provisão *nf* provisions
provisionar *vt* to provision
provisioneiro *nm* purveyor
puba *nf* macerated cassava
pubo *a* [Braz] fermented
púcara (púcaro *nm) nf* cup; mug
pudim *nm* pudding; flan; **~ de leite** caramel pudding; (of fish) balls; **~ de pão** bread pudding
pulmão *nm* lung
pulverizado *a* powdered
pulverizar *vt* to powder
purê *nm* purée; **~ de batata** mashed potatoes
purgueira *nf* pine tree seed
puri *nm* [Braz] cassava variety
purunga (purungo *nm) nf* calabash gourd
pururuca *nf* [Braz] (of coconut) crumbly
putrefato (putrefeito) *a* rotten
putrião (pato bravo) *nm* (of duck) mallard
pútrido *a* putrid
puxar *vt* to heat
puxavante *nm* well-seasoned food

Q

q.b. (quanto basta) *abbr* (of flavouring &c) add-to-taste
quadra *nf* (of time) season
quadril *nm* (of beef) rump
quadro-negro *nm* blackboard
qualidade *nf* quality
qualificação *nf* (of standard) qualification
qualificado *a* (of standard) qualified
quantidade *nf* quantity
quarta-feira *nf* Wednesday
quartear *vt* to quarter; to divide into four
quartilho *nm* (of measure) pint
quartinha *nf* [Braz] jug
quarto *nm* (of proportion) quarter; (of meat) joint
quartola *nf* cask
quatro *nm* (of number) four
quebra *nf* breakage; break; **~-nozes** nutcrackers; **~-queixo** cheap cigar
quebradiço *a* friable; breakable
quebrado *a* broken
quebrar *vt* (of fast &c) to break
queijada *nf* cheesecake
queijadeira (~o *nm) nf* cheese-cake seller
queijadinha *nf* (of confectionery) coconut sweet
queijar *vt* to make cheese
queijaria *nf* (of cheese) dairy
queijeira *nf* cheese mould; **(~o** *nm)* (of person) cheese-maker/seller
queijo *nm* cheese; **~ duro (mineiro)** hard cheese; **~ de Évora** semi-hard unpasteurized ewe's milk cheese; **~ fresco (~ mole)**

soft cheese; ~ **gorgonzola** gorgonzola cheese; ~ **da Ilha** parmesan-like cheese; ~ **de Nisa** (semi-)/hard ewe's milk cheese; ~ **parmesão** Parmesan cheese; ~ **prato** [Braz] Edam-like cheese; ~ **ralado** grated cheese; ~ **de São Jorge** (semi-)/hard crumbly cow's milk cheese; ~ **da Serra** soft ewe's milk cheese; ~ **suíço** gruyère cheese; ~ **tipo cheddar** cheddar cheese

queijoso (caseoso) *a* cheesy

queimada *nf* brandy variety

queimado *nm* [Braz] (of confectionery) burnt-sugar sweet; burnt smell

queimão *a* (of red pepper) piquant

queimar *vt* to burn; to toast

queimo *nm* piquant taste

queimoso *a* piquant; hot

queixa *nf* complaint

queixada *nf* wild boar

quela *nf* (of crustacean) claw; pincer

quenga *nf* okra-ed chicken stew; [Braz] (of vessel) coconut cup

quentão *nm* [Braz] hot rum/ginger/cloves/cinnamon/sugar; hot alcoholic drink

quente *a* (of temperature) hot

queque *nm* cake

queto (quieto) *a* quiet

quiabo *nm* okra; **~-cheiroso** [Braz] musk mallow

quibando (quibano) *nm* [Braz] sieve

quibe *nm* wholemeal flour/deep-fried minced-meat/flour/onion/salt/mint dish

quibebe *nm* pumpkin purée

quiçamã *nm* [Braz] cassava starch paste

quigombô (quigombó) *nf* [Braz] okra

quilo *nm* kilo

quilograma *nm* kilogram

quilômetro *nm* kilometer

quimanga *nf* (of vessel) coconut-shell container

quimbombô (quimbombó) ([Braz] **quiabo)** *nm* okra

quina *nf* quinine

quinado *nm* quinined wine

quinanga *nf* wooden food bucket

quindão *nm* (of confectionery) large coconut sweet

quindim *nm* [Braz] (of confectionery) small coconut sweet

quinecu *nm* [Braz] rice variety

quinta *nf* farm; estate; **~-essência (quintessência)** quintessence; **~-feira** Thursday; ~ **dos Videis** semi-hard goat cheese

quinzena *nf* fortnight

quioiô *nm* [Braz] sweet basil

quiosque *nm* kiosk

quitação (quitança) (quitamento *nm) nf*

repayment
quitanda *nf* greengrocer's
quitandar *vt* to sell fruit/ vegetables
quitandê *nm* [Braz] small green beans
quitandeiro *nm* (of person) greengrocer
quitute *nm* [Braz] tasty appetizer; titbit
quituteiro *nm* [Braz] (of person) titbit-maker

R

rã *nf* frog; **~ gigante-touro** bullfrog
rabaçal *nm* semi-hard ewe or goat cheese
rabaçaria *nf* vegetables; greens; (of fruit) seconds
rabada *nf* braised oxtail
rabanada *nf* French toast
rabanete *nm* radish
rábano *nm* turnip; **~ picante (~ rústico) (~ silvestre)** horseradish
rabilo *nm* sea fish: bluefin tuna
rabo *nm* (of fish &c) tail; **~-aberto** yellow-tailed snapper; **~-de-galo** cocktail
racionamento *nm* ration
racionar *vt* to ration; to apportion
rafado *a* hungry; starved
ragu *nm* ragout
raia *nf* (of fish) skate
raineto *nf* (of apple) cox's orange (queen)
rainha *nf* queen bee; apple/pear variety; **~-cláudia** greengage; **~-dos-prados** (of herb) meadowsweet
raiz *nf* root; (of celery) stick; **~-doce** licorice
rala *nf* bran; brown flour; **pão de ~** brown bread
ralado *a* grated
ralador *nm* grater
raladura *nf* grating
ralar *vt* to grate
ralo *nm* grater
ramalhete *nm* bouquet; (of flowers) bunch
ramo *nm* bouquet; bunch of flowers; branch; **~ de cheiros** bouquet garni
rançar (rancescer) *vi* to go stale
rancheiro *nm* army cook; mess-mate
rangifer (rangifero) *nm* reindeer; caribou
rapadura *nf* raw brown sugar loaf; (of sweet) sugar-cane
rapaz *nm* (of bird) snipe
rapé *nm* snuff
rapioca *nf* beanfeast; lavish meal
rapistro *nm* wild turnip variety
rapôncio (raponço) *nm* (of herb) rampion
rascância *nf* (of wine) dryness; sharpness
rascante *nm* (of wine) plonk; *a* (of taste) tart

rascasso *nm* sea fish: scorpion fish; rockfish
rasga-mortalha *nf* [Braz] Praguayan snipe
raspa *nf* slice; zest; (of lemon &c) peel; (of confectionery) piece of candy
raspado *a* (of nutmeg &c) grated
ratafia *nf* ratafia; fruit-stone spirits
ravióli *nm* (of pasta) ravioli
real *a* royal
rebaixa *nf* (of price) reduction
rebaixado *a* (of price) reduced
rebaixador *nm* cut-price merchant
rebaixar *vt* to reduce the price
rebotalho *nm* crumbs; scraps; left-overs
rebuçado *nm* lollipop; (of confectionery) wrapped sweet
recalcador *nm* wine-press
receber *vt* (of hosting) to receive; to entertain; to welcome
recebimento *nm* reception; wedding
receita *nm* recipe; **livro de ~s de cozinha** cookbook
recém-posto *a* (of egg) new-laid; fresh laid
recepção *nf* reception; **sala de ~** drawing-room
recepcionar *vt* (of guests) to receive; to give a party
recepcionista *nm/f* [Braz] receptionist
receptáculo *nm* receptacle
recheado *nm* stuffing; *a* full; stuffed
recheadura *nf* stuffing
rechear *vt* to stuff
recheio *nm* (of turkey &c) stuffing; filling
recheios *nm* dressing
recipiente *nm* receptacle; **~ de armazenagem** storage bin; **~ de barro** terrine
recocto *a* re-cooked; over-cooked
recomendado *a* recommended
recozer *vt* to re-cook; to over-cook
recozido *a* re-cooked; over-cooked
recozimento *nm* cooking; over-cooking
redestilar *vt* to re-distil
redução *nf* (of price) cut
reduzir *vt* (of sauce &c) to reduce; to thicken; to grind; (of price) to cut, to reduce
reespumas *nf* [Braz] sugar variety
refeição *nf* meal
refeitório *nm* refectory
referver *vt* to reboil
refervido *a* reboiled
refinado *a* (of sugar &c) refined
refinar *vt* (of sugar &c) to refine; to purify; to clarify
refinaria *nf* (of sugar &c) refinery

refogado *nm* gravy; butter-sauce; dish cooked in butter; stew; *a* sautéed

refogar *vt* to fry in butter/oil onioned/herbed; to simmer

refratário (refrativo) *a* (of dishes &c) ovenproof

refrescamento *nm* refreshment

refrescante *a* refreshing

refrescar *vt* to cool; to refrigerate; (of temperature) to drop

refresco *nm* refreshment

refrigeração *nf* refrigeration; cooling; freezing

refrigerador *nm* refrigerator; freezer; ice-box; *a* cooling

refrigerante *nm* refreshment; cooling soft drink; refrigeration

refrigerar *vt* to cool; to chill

refrigeratório *a* cooling

refrigério *nm* refrigeration; freezing

regada *nf* farm

regalado *a* delicious

regalão *nm* epicurean; gourmet; gastronome

regalar *vt* to feast; to entertain;

regalona *nf* (of tree) olive variety; (of tree) plum variety

regar *vt* (of roasting) to baste; to wet; to moisten; (of meal with drink) to wash down

regelar *vt* to re-freeze

região *nf* region

regime *nm* (of food) diet

Reguengos de Monsaraz *nm* Alentejo vineyard

regulador *nm* (of oven temperature &c) control; regulo

regular *vt* (of oven temperature &c) to control; to regulate

reima *nf* olive juice

reincorporar *vt* to blend-in

relangueiro *nm* sea fish: oarfish

relish *nm* relish; **~ de pepino** cucumber relish

relógio *nm* clock

remela *nf* [Braz] coconut pulp

reminhol *nm* large copper spoon

remoído *nm* [Braz] bran

remolada *nf* spicy sauce

rendimento *nm* (of harvest) crop

renova *nf* shoot; sprout

renovo *nm* vegetable garden

repartir meio por meio *vt* (of payment) to go dutch

repastar *vt* to feed; to feast

repasto *nm* repast; substantial meal

repimpado *a* well-fed

repimpar *vt* (of food) to satisfy

repisa *nf* (of wine) last pressing

repolga *nf* chestnut mushroom

repolho *nm* cabbage; **~ chinês** Chinese cabbage; **~ crespo** kale; **~ roxo** Scottish kale; red cabbage; **salada de ~ cru** coleslaw

repostaria *nf* kitchen utensils;

pastry room
reposteiro *nm* butler
requeijão *nm* cottage cheese; cheese-spread
requeime *nm* piquant-flavour
requentado *a* (of food) re-heated
requentão *nm* (of whisky/ brandy) laced coffee
requentar *vt* (of food) to re-heat
requerer *vt* (of waiter) to request; to ask for
rês *nf* cattle; **~ assada** barbecue
rés-do-chão *nm* ground floor; first floor [USA]
rescaldeiro (rescaldo) *nm* chafing-dish; hot-plate
reserva *nf* (of table) reservation
reservado *nm* (of table) reserved
reservar *vt* (of table) to reserve; (of cooking) set aside
resfriadeira *nf* (of cool water) earthenware jug
resfriado *a* cold; chilled; iced
resfriador (resfriadouro) *nm* refrigerator
resfriar *vt* to cool; to freeze
resguardo *nm* diet
resíduo *nm* dregs; grounds; lees; (of spirits) marc
ressaibo *nm* (of savour) bad taste
ressalgada *nf* salted meat
ressentido *a* (of fruit) going off
ressequido *a* withered
ressuar *vt* to sweat
restaurante *nm* restaurant; café; **~ automático** food vending-machine
réstia *nf* (of onions &c) string
restilo *nm* [Braz] brandy; spirits
restos *nmpl* (of meal) remains; scraps
retalhar *vt* to cut-up; to chine; to chop
retalheiro *nm* (of shop) retailer
retalho *nm* small piece; slice; scrap
retame *nm* molasses; treacle
reter-se *vi* to abstain
retirar *vt* (of giblets &c) to remove; to take out
retreta *nf* WC
reunião *nf* reunion; party; **~ de homens** stag-party; **~ de senhoras (~ de mulheres)** hen-party;
revedor *nm* [Braz] (of water) well
reveillon *nm* new year's eve party
revirado *nm* [Braz] (of dish) cassava/maize with beans and meat/fish
rexenxão *nm* blackbird variety
ria *nf* estuary
riachão *nm* river; stream
ribafria *nm* peppered semi-hard goat cheese
riboflavina *nf* riboflavin
rico *a* (of ingredient) rich

ricota *nf* (of cottage cheese) ricotta; cream-cheese
rilhar *vt* to chew
rim (rins *pl) nm* kidney
ringir *vt* to chew
rio *nm* river
ripada *nf* [Braz] (of brandy) drop
risoto *nm* risotto
rissole *nm* rissole
robalo *nm* nm sea fish: snook; sea bass; white perch
rocambole *nm* pastry-roll; swiss roll; **~ recheado com creme de limão** swiss roll with lemon-curd filling
rochina *nf* [Braz] manioc variety
rocinha *nf* farm
rodada *nf* (of drinks) round
rodela *nf* slice
rodileira *nf* [Braz] sea fish: caribe; piranha
rodilha *nf* dish-cloth
rodízio *nm* (of restaurant) carvery
rodovalho *nm* sea fish: turbot; brill
rodoviária *nf* [Braz] bus station
roer *vt* to nibble; to chew
rojão *nm* crackling
rola *nf* turtle dove
roleira *nf* candlestick
rolete *nm* peeled sugar-cane
rolha *nf* cork; stopper; **tirar a ~** to uncork; (of bottle) to open
rolhar *vt* (of bottle) to stopper; to cork
rolim *nm* sea fish: sunfish
rolinho *nm* small roll
rolo *nm* (of pastry) rolling-pin; taper; candle; roll
romã *nf* pomegranate
romeiro *nm* sea fish: horse mackerel; pilot fish
roncador *nm* sea fish: hogfish; pigfoot; grunt
rondelli *nm* cannelloni
roquefort *nm* (of cheese) Roquefort, blue ewe's milk cheese
rosa-almiscarada *nf* abelmosk, abelmusk
rosado *a* (of wine) rosé
rosassolis *nm* (of liqueur) rosa solis
rosbife *nm* roast beef
rosca *nf* (of bread) twist; fried-cake [USA]
roseta *nf* rosette
rosmaninho *nm* (of herb) rosemary
rosquilha (rosquilho *nm) nf* ring-shaped biscuit; doughnut
rosquinha *nf* jelly doughnut
roupa *nf* clothes; **~ de banho (~ para praia)** bathing costume (things); **~ de mesa** table-linen; **~-velha** left-overs stew; cassava/beans/minced-meat dish
roupeiro *nm* cheese-maker
roxo-forte *nm* [Braz] brandy; rum
rua *nf* street; **~ comercial** shopping street; **~ principal** high street

rubiácea *nf* [Braz] coffee plant; coffee
rubo *nm* blackberry
rúcula *nf* (of salad) rocket
ruiharbo *nm* rhubarb, pieplant
ruivaca *nf* freshwater fish: roach
ruivo *nm* sea fish: gurnard
rum *nm* rum
ruptura *nf* breakage
rutabaga *nf* rutabaga, swede

S

sábado *nm* Saturday
sabão *nm* soap; **~-de-soldado** soapberry
sabável *a* [Braz] tasty; savoury
sabiá *nm* [Braz] song-thrush
sabor *nm* flavour; taste; **~ restante** after-taste
saborear *vt* to savour; to taste
saboroso *a* savoury; tasty; delicious
sabugo *nm* corncob
sabugueiro *nm* [Braz] (of tree) elder; **~ d'água** (of plant) cranberry
saca-rolhas *nm* corkscrew
sacarina *nf* saccharin
saciar *vt* (of hunger/thirst) to satisfy; to quench
saco (saca *nf) nm* bag; sack; (of coffee) filter-bag; **~ de papel** paper bag
sacolejar *vt* (of liquid) to shake
sacudir *vt* to shake
safio *nm* conger eel
safra *nf* harvest; crop
sagu *nm* sago
sagum *nm* sago variety
saí *nm* (of monkey) capuchin
saibo *nm* taste; flavour
saicanga (ueua) (peixe-cachorro) *nf* [Braz] freshwater fish: saicanga
saída *nf* exit; **~ de emergência** emergency exit
saieta *nf* [Braz] (of drink) fermented coconut
saiga *nf* antelope
saijé (saipé) *nm* sea fish: dorado
sair *vt* to leave; to go
saíra *nf* blackbird variety
sal *nm* salt; **~ de cozinha** cooking salt; **~ gema** rock-salt; **~ grosso** coarse salt; **~ marinho** sea-salt; **~ mineral** mineral salt; **~ refinado** table salt; **sem ~** salt-free; without salt
sala *nf* large room; **~ de café** coffee-room; **~ de espera** waiting-room; **~ de estar** living-room; **~ de jantar** dining-room; **~ de recepcão** (of room) reception; **~ de visitas** drawing-room
salada *nf* salad; **~ de alface** lettuce salad; **~ completa** lettuce/tomato/carrot/palm heart/potato/onion/olives/ham/cheese salad; **~ de batata** potato salad; **~ de frango** chicken salad; **~ de frutas**

fruit salad; **~ de frutos-do-mar** seafood salad; **~ mista** mixed salad; **óleo para ~** salad-oil; **tempero para ~** salad-dressing; **~ de tomate** tomato salad; **~ verde** mixed green salad; **~ waldorf** waldorf salad

saladeira *nf* salad-bowl

salamé *nm* salami

salaminho *nm* salami variety

salão *nm* salon; **~ de café** coffee-shop; **~ de festas** banqueting hall; **~ de baile** ball-room

saleiro *nm* salt-cellar; **~ moedor** (of table) salt-mill

salema *nf* sea fish: porkfish; sea bream

salepo *nm* salep

saleta *nf* sitting-room; hall; waiting-room

salga (salgação, salgadura) *nf* pickling; salting; curing

salgadinhos *nm* [Braz] salty appetizers; **~ de queijo** cheese-straws

salgado *a* salty; pickled; briny; **água ~a** salt water

salgadura *nf* salting; curing

salgar *vt* to salt; to cure; to pickle; to kipper

salinidade *nf* saltiness

salmão *nm* salmon; **~ defumado** smoked salmon; **~ novo** grilse; **~-rei** blueback salmon; **~-rosa** pink salmon; **~ salgado e defumado** kipper; **~-truta** sea-trout; **~-vermelho** sockeye salmon

salmonete *nm* sea fish: red mullet; goatfish

salmoura *nf* brine

salmourar *vt* to brine; to pickle

saloio *nm* ewe's milk cheese

saloneiro *nm* [Braz] (of ship) steward

salpicado *a* salt-sprinkled

salpicão *nm* pork-pie; smoked ham or pork sausage; **~ de vinhais** smoked red wine/garlic spiced pork sausage

salpicar (salpintar) *vt* to sprinkle; to salt; to corn

salpico *nm* sprinkling; drop

salpimenta *nf* salt/pepper-mix

salpimentar *vt* (of salt and pepper) to season

salpresar *vt* to lightly salt

salpreso *a* salted; corned

salsa *nf* parsley; salsa; **~-americana** sarsaparilla; **~ da-rocha** stone parsley; **~ verde** salsa verde; herb-thickened vinaigrette

salsão *nm* celery

salsaparrilha (salsa-americana) *nf* sarsaparilla

salseira *nf* sauce-boat; saucer

salsicha *nf* sausage; hot-dog; **~ alemã (~ de cachorro-quente)** frankfurter

salsichão *nm* large sausage

salsicharia *nf* (of pork) butcher's

salsinha *nf* parsley

saltear *vt* to sauté
salva (salveta) (sálvia) *nf* sage
samburá *nm* [Braz] wicker fish-basket
samanguaiá *nm* (of mollusc) clam
sambongo *nm* (of confectionery) coconut sweet
samovar *nm* samovar; tea urn
san jorge *nm* cow's milk cheese
sandes *nf* sandwich
sandilho *nm* sea fish: sandeel
sanduíche *nm* sandwich; burger; **~ americano** [Braz] ham and fried egg
sanfeno *nm* fenugreek
sangra *nf* pressed-olives liquid
sangria *nf* negus; hot wine/water/sugar
sangue *nm* blood
sant'ana *nf* [Braz] July
santarém *nm* goat cheese
santola *nf* spider-crab
são *nm* (of food) healthy
sapateira *nf* crab
sapatinho-do-diabo *nm* [Braz] nasturtium
sápido *a* savoury
sapota *nf* [Braz] sapote, marmelade tree
sapoti *nm* [Braz] sapodilla
saquê *nm* sake
saquim *nm* kosher butcher's knife
saquinho *nm* (of paper &c) bag
saramago *nm* wild radish
sarau *nm* soirée
sarça *nf* bramble
sarcocárpio *nm* sarcocarp, fleshy-part of fruit
sarda (serra-comum) (bonito) *nf* sea fish: mackerel; bonito; skipjack tuna
sardinela *nf* freshwater fish: sardinella
sardinha *nf* sardine; pilchard; **~ de conserva** tinned sardines
sardinhão (apapá) (dorada) *nm* [Braz] freshwater fish: Amazonion herring
sardinheiro *nm* sardine-seller
sardinopa *nm* sea fish: pilchards
sargo *nm* sea fish: sea bream
sarigüê *nm* opossum
sarrabulho *nm* pork stew
sarrajão *nm* sea fish: bonito
sarsapatel *nm* haggis
saruê (gambá) *nm* opossum; ear of corn
sashimi *nm* sashimi
sassafrás *nm* [Braz] sassafras
satisfazer *vt* (of hunger &c) to satisfy
saturado *a* soaked-in; saturated
saturar *vt* to saturate
saudação *nf* greeting; welcome
saudade *nf* [Braz] greeting to absent friend(s)
saudar *vt* to greet; to salute
saúde! *nf* cheers! your health!
saúna *nf* [Braz] small white mullet

savel *nm* freshwater fish: shad
savelha *nf* little shad
sazão *nf* season; **sem ~ (fora da ~)** out of season
sazonado *a* (of fruit) ripened
sazonamento *nm* ripening
sazonar *vt* to season; to ripen
sebereba ([Braz] **chibé, jacuba)** *nf* cassava/(rum) drink
sebo *nm* suet; (of candle) tallow
seboso *a* suety
secador *nm* (of coffee beans &c) drier; washing-up rack
secar *vt* to dry; to kipper
seco *a* dry; (of people) thirsty; **meio ~** (of wine) demi-sec; **muito ~** (of wine) brut; **pão ~** unbuttered bread; **~ ao sol** sun-dried; *nmpl* **~s** dry foods; groceries
sede *nf* thirst; dryness
sedimento *nm* dregs; lees; sediment
segmento *nm* segment
segunda-feira *nf* Monday
segundo *nm* second; **pão de ~a** brown bread
segurelha *nf* (of herb) savory
seis *nm* (of number) six
sela *nf* (of meat) saddle
selecionar *vt* to choose
seleta *nf* pear variety; orange variety
selim *nm* [Goa] bunch of coconuts
sem *prep* (of alcohol/ effervescence &c) free; **~ gordura** fat-free; **~-sal** unsalted
semana *nf* week; **próxima ~** next week; **~ passada** last week; **~ seguinte** following week
sêmea *nf* bran; bran-bread
semente *nf* (of caraway &c) seed
semiduro *a* (of cheese &c) semi-soft
sêmola (semolina) *nf* semolina
senga *nf* [Braz] left-overs; bran; (of molluscs) shell
senhor *nm* Mr
senhora *nf* Mrs
senhorinha ([Braz] **senhorita)** *nf* Miss
sensabor *nm* tasteless; flavourless
sensaboria *nf* lack of taste; lack of flavour
sentar *vt* to seat; **~-se** to sit down
senuca *nf* sea fish: tunny
separador *nm* milk-skimmer
separar *vt* to separate
sequilho *nm* cracknel; crisp biscuit
serão *nm* soirée
sercial *nm* (of wine) dry light madeira
sereia *nf* sea fish: pompano
sereíba *nf* [Braz] Indian fig
sernambiguara ([Braz] **tambó)** *nm* round pompano

serpa *nm* sweet oily ewe's milk cheese

serra *nf* sea fish: bonito; **~-garoupa** sea fish: grouper variety; **~ da estrela** buttery rich ewe's milk cheese

serrano *nm* goat cheese; smoked ham

sertã (sartã) *nf* frying-pan

sérum *nm* whey

servente *nm* servant

serviço *nm* service; set of dishes; cover-charge; **~ incluído** service charge included; **~ não incluído** not including service charge; **~ de mesa** dinner service; **~ de prata** silverware canteen

servidor *nm* attendant

servir *vt* to serve; (of table) to wait **~ à mesa** to serve up a meal; **~ o chá** to pour out the tea

sésamo *nm* sesame

sete *nm* (of number) seven; **~ barbas** [Braz] leather-fish

setembro *nm* September

Setúbal *nm* wine-growing region

sevilhana *nf* olive variety

sexta-feira *nf* Friday

shitake *nm* (of mushroom) shitake

siba *nf* cuttle-fish

sicite *nf* fig-wine

sicuri *nm* shark variety

sidra *nf* cider

sifão *nm* syphon

siluro *nm* freshwater fish: sheatfish

silva *nf* blackberry

silveira *nf* [Braz] (of dish) chopped meat

sineta *nf* small bell

sinhaninha *nf* white rum

sinimbu *nm* iguana

sintético *a* synthetic

sipia *nf* white rum

sirage *nm* sesame oil

siri *nm* crab; **casquinha de ~** crab au gratin

siricaia *nf* [Braz] (of dish) milk/sugar/eggs

sirigóia *nm* [Braz] saltwater crab

siriri *nm* [Braz] mussel variety

sirizada *nf* [Braz] crab delicacy

siroposo *a* syrupy

sitarrão *nm* big ranch/farm

sitioca *nf* [Braz] small ranch/farm

sito *nm* mould; mildew

smoking *nm* dinner-jacket; tuxedo

soalheiro *a* (of position) sunny

sobejo *nm* leftovers; candle-end

soborralho *a* baked in embers

sobras *nf* offal

sobreano *nm* calf

sobrecostilhar *nm* [Braz] rib of beef

sobreloja *nf* mezzanine

sobremesa *nf* pudding; dessert; topping; coffee; (of confectionery) sweets

sobrenome *nm* surname
sobrepaga *nf* gratuity; tip
sobriedade *nf* sobriety
sóbrio *a* sober
socar *vt* to knead
socializar *vi* to socialize
soda *nf* soda-water; **~ cáustica** caustic soda; **~ limonada** lemon squash
sofá *nf* (of restaurant) padded bench
soirée *nf* soirée
soja *nm* soy
sol *nm* sun; **ressecado pelo ~** sun-dried
sola *nf* (of confectionery) cassava sweet
solha *nf* sea fish: plaice; **~-limão** lemon sole; **~ dos mares do norte** dab; **~-de-pedras** flounder; **~-reis** sturgeon; **~ da rocha** rock sole
solhão *nm* sea fish: flounder; dab
solho *nm* sea fish: sturgeon
solúvel *a* soluble
sombrinha *nf* parasol; sunshade
sonho *nm* doughnut
sopa *nf* soup; broth; soup-dunked bread; **~ de aveia** oatmeal soup; **~ de clame** clam chowder; **~ do dia** soup of the day; **~ juliana** julienne; **~ de mariscos** seafood soup; **~ de mexilhões** mussel soup; **~ de ostra** oyster stew; **~ de tomate** tomato soup; **~ de verduras** vegetable soup
sopeira *nf* soup tureen
sopetarra *nf* rich soup; snack
sopetear *vt* to dunk; to savour
sopista *nm* (of person) soup-lover
soquete *nm* [Braz] stew
sorda *nf* cassava/egg/beef soup
sorgo *nm* sorghum; **~-doce** sorgo, sweet sorghum
soro *nm* whey
sororoca *nf* [Braz] sea fish: Spanish mackerel
sortido *nm* assortment; *a* assorted
sortimento *nm* assortment
sorva *nf* fruit of rowan tree
sorvado (sorval) *a* (of fruit) over-ripe
sorvar *vi* (of fruit) to start to go off
sorver *vt* to sip
sorvete *nm* ice; sorbet; ice-cream; **~ de café** iced coffee; **~ com chantilly** ice-cream with cream; **~ de creme** vanilla ice-cream; **~ cremoso** ice-cream; **~ de flocos** chocolate-chip ice-cream **~ de frutas** tutti-frutti; **~ de suco de fruta com água e açúcar** water ice; **vendedor de ~** ice-cream-man
sorveteira *nf* ice-cream maker; freezer

sorveteiro *nm* ice-cream-man
sovadura *nf* kneading
sovar *vt* to knead; (of grapes) to tread
suã *nf* loin of pork
suaçuapara *nm* [Braz] white-spotted deer
suaçupita *nm* [Braz] red deer
suaçutinga *nm* [Braz] small deer variety
suadouro *nm* (of kitchenware) washing
suar *vt* to distil; (of cooking) to sweat; *nm* butternut tree
suave *a* (of wine) smooth
suavidade *nf* (of wine) smoothness
suba *nf* [Braz] price-increase
subcinerício *a* baked-in-embers
submergir *vt* to cover with water &c
subsolo *nm* basement
substância *nf* (of food elements) goodness; **~ conservadora** (of food) preservative
substancial *a* nourishing
substanciar *vt* to feed; to nourish
substancioso *a* nourishing; nutritive
subterrâneo *nm* basement
sucedâneo *a* substitute; ersatz
suco *nm* juice; **~ de frutas** fruit juice; **~ de laranja** orange juice; **~ de limão** lemon juice; **~ de maçã** apple juice; **~ de pêssego** peach juice; **~ de tomate** tomato juice; **~ de uva** grape juice
suculência *nf* juiciness
suculento (sucoso) *a* juicy; succulent
sucursal *nf* chain-store
sucutuba *a* juicy; succulent
suflê *nm* soufflé; **~ de queijo** cheese soufflé
sujar *vt* (of tablecloth &c) to mark; to stain
sukiyaki *nm* sukiyaki
sumaca *nf* jerked beer
sumarento (sumoso) *a* juicy; succulent
sumo (suco) *nm* juice; **~-da-cana** [Braz] sugar-cane brandy; white rum
sumpção (sunção) *nf* (of drinking) swallow
suor-de-alambique *nm* [Braz] sugar-cane brandy; white rum; liquor
superior *nm* (of quality &c) superior
supermercado *nm* supermarket
suplantar *vt* (of grapes) to tread
suporte *nm* knife-stand
sura *nf* fermented palm juice
surubim (cachara) (pintado) *nm* freshwater fish: stripped catfish
sururu *nm* [Braz] mollusc: clam
sushi *nm* sushi
suspender *vt* (of game) to

hang
suspiro *nm* (of confectionery) sugared egg-white sweet; macaroon
sustento *nm* sustenance
sutinga *nf* [Braz] cassava variety

T

tabacaria *nf* tobacconist's
tabaco *nm* tobacco
tabaquear *nm* (of tobacco) to smoke; to take snuff
tabarana (tubarana) (dourado-branco) *nf* freshwater fish: tabarana
tabefe *nm* egg-nog; whey
tabela *nf* (of prices) list
tabelado *a* fixed-price
taberna *nf* pub; tavern; inn
taberneiro *nm* publican; inn-keeper
tablete *nm* (of chocolate) bar; (of butter) pat
taboca (taquara) *nf* [Braz] bamboo
tábua *nm* (of chopping) board; (of table) leaf
tabuleiro *nm* cake-tin
taca *nf* arrowroot
taça *nf* cup; wine glass; goblet
tacacá *nm* tapioca/cassava/shrimp/garlic/chili dish
tacaré *nm* [Braz] cassava variety
tachada *nf* potful
tacho *nm* pot; pan; bowl; (of wine) glass
taco *nm* taco
tacomaré *nm* [Braz] sugar cane variety
tacuité (queixada *nf) nm* [Braz] wild boar
tacuru (tacurua *nf)* **(tacuruba** *nf) nm* [Braz] (of outdoor cooking) trivet of stones
tafía (cachaça *nf) nm* rum variety
tafulho *nm* (of bottle) cork; stopper
tagetes *nm* French marigold
tágico *a* (of river) Tagus
tagliatelle *nm* tagliatelle
taguicati (queixada *nf) nm* wild boar
tainha *nf* sea fish: mullet
taioba *nf* (of vegetable) taioba
taipeiro *nm* [Braz] mixed plateful
taititu *nm* [Braz] wild boar
taiuiá *nm* pumpkin; squash
tajacica *nf* freshwater fish: perch variety
talagada *nf* [Braz] (of alcohol) gulp
talão de cheques *nm* cheque-book
talha *nf* large earthenware dish
talhada *nf* slice; (of confectionery) cassava/brown-sugar sweet
talhador *nm* cleaver; *a* cutting; chopping
talhão *nm* large earthenware water jar

talharim *nm* noodle; vermicelli
talher *nm* cruet-stand; place-setting; **~es** cutlery; tableware
talho (talhamento) *nm* (of meat) cut; cutting; butcher's; butcher's block
talo *nm* stalk
tâmara *nf* (of fruit) date
tamarindo (tamarindeiro) (tamarineiro) (tamarinheiro) (jubai) (tamarineira *nf) nm* tamarind
tamaru *nm* [Braz] mantis shrimp
tamarutaca (lagosta-gafanhoto) (mãe-de-camarão) (tambarutaca) (tamburutaca) *nm* mantis shrimp
tamati *nm* [Braz] cockle
tamba *nf* [Braz] fermented tapioca drink
tambaqui *nm* [Braz] freshwater fish: tambaqui; pacu
tambeira *nf* [Braz] heifer
tambo *nm* [Braz] cattle farm
tambona *nf* [Braz] coffee pot
tamboril (diabo-marinho) *nm* sea fish: angler fish; monkfish
tampa *nf* lid; cover; cork; stopper; covering
tampado *a* covered; stopped
tampão *nm* large lid; (of barrel) bung
tampar *vt* to cover; to stopper
tamponar *vt* to stopper
tangar *vt* (of dance) to tango
tangerina *nm* mandarin
taniça *nf* pig-tail tobacco
tanino *nm* tannin
tapa (linguado-lixa) *nf* [Braz] tongue-fish
tapador *nm* lid; cork
tapar *vt* to cork; to close; to lid; to cover
taperebá (cajá) *nm* [Braz] (of tree) cashew variety
tapiara *nf* [Braz] mullet variety
tapicuri *nm* [Braz] cassava wine
tapioca *nf* tapioca; (of confectionery) coconut/tapioca sweet
tapiocuí *nm* cassava starch
tapiriba *nf* [Braz] (of fruit) yellow plum
taqueira *nf* [Braz] small flat pumpkin
taralhão *nm* (of mullusc) piddock
tarambola *nf* golden plover
taranja (toronja) *nf* grapefruit
taraxaco *nm* dandelion
tarde *nf* afternoon; evening; **boa ~!** good afternoon! good evening!
tardio *a* late
targana (tainha) *nf* mullet variety
tari *nm* palm juice liquor
tarifa *nf* tariff; (of tax) duty
tarpão (camurupim) (pirapema) (pema) *nm* sea fish: tarpon; silverfish
tarraçada *nf* (of drink) bowlful
tartárico *a* tartaric

tarte *nm* tart
tartizar *vt* to tartarize
tarubá *nf* (of drink) fermented tapioca
tasca (tasco) *nf/m* pub; tavern
tascar *vt* (of food sample) to share
tasqueiro *nm* publican; inn-keeper
tatu *nm* armadillo; [Braz] pig variety
tatuaíva *nm* [Braz] armadillo
taverna *nf* inn; pub; tavern
táxi *nm* taxi; **chamar um ~** to hail a taxi; **ponto (de estacionamento) de ~s** taxi-rank
teácea *nf* (of plant) tea bush
teáceo *a* tea
teatro *nm* theatre
teimoso *nf* spirits; rum
teiroga *nm* sea fish: white skate
telefone *nm* telephone; **~ público** public call box
televisão *nf* television; video
telho *nm* earthenware cover
têmpera *nf* seasoning; spice; temperature
temperado *a* seasoned; spicy
temperar *vt* to season; to spice
temperatura (tempérie) *nf* temperature
tempero *nm* seasoning; spice; dressing; flavour; taste
tempo *nm* time; weather
tenca *nf* freshwater fish: tench
tendão *nm* tendon; sinew
tender *vt* (of bread) to mould
tenro *a* (of meat &c) tender
tentáculo *nm* tentacle
tento-pequeno *nm* Indian licorice
teor alcohólico *nm* alcoholic content
tépido *a* lukewarm; tepid
tequila *nf* tequila
ter *vt* to contain
terçã-feira (terçã) *nf* Tuesday; **~ gorda** Shrove Tuesday
terebintina *nf* [Braz] spirits; rum
terecaí *nm* turtle
teriaga *nf* treacle
terminal *nm* (of station) terminal
termo *nm* vacuum flask
termômetro *nm* thermometer
terneiro *nm* [Braz] calf
terra *nf* land; ground; earth; **da ~** local
terraço *nm* terrace; roof-terrace
terrantês *nm* green grape variety
terrina *nf* soup tureen; (of sauce) gravy-boat; **~ de peixe** fish pie
terrincho *nm* ewe's milk cheese
tesoura (tesoira) *nf* scissors; **~s** cutlery; fiddler crab; (of crab &c) claw
testo *nm* lid
tetipoteira *nf* grape variety
tetraz-pequeno-das-serras

nm black-grouse; capercaillie
tiambo *nm* [Braz] sugar-cane
tiborna *nf* oil-dunked hot bread; plonk
ticaca (gambá) *nf* [Braz] opossum
ticonha *nf* [Braz] sea fish: skate variety
ticuanga *nf* coconut/cassava/chesnut cake
tigela *nf* cup; bowl; porringer; dish; [Braz] litre
tigelada *nf* bowlful; lemon/honey pudding
tigelinha *nf* cream puff
tilápia *nf* freshwater fish: tilapia
timalo *nm* migratory fish: grayling
timbale *nm* sea fish: needlefish
timbó-do-rio-de-janeiro (canapu) *nm* [Braz] ground cherry
timbu *nm* [Braz] opossum
timo *nm* thyme
timucu *nm* [Braz] sea fish: needlefish
tinelo *nm* staff dining-room
tinote *nm* vat
tinquinho *nm* (of quantity) pinch; dash
tinta *nf* grape variety; (of squid &c) ink
tinto *a* (of wine) red; **~ aloirado** ruby
tintureiro *nm* grape variety
tiquara *nf* cassava drink
tiquíra *nf* cassava spirits
tira-gosto *nm* savoury; snack; salty canapé
tirar *vt* to draw off; to remove; to extract; to skim-off
tiravira *nm* sea fish: lizard fish
tisana *nf* tisane
titela *nf* (of fowl) breast
tiúba *nf* spirits; rum
toalha *nf* towel; cloth; (of table) tablecloth
toasta *nf* toast
tócal *nm* Tokay
tocar *vt* (of glasses) to chink; to clink
tocari *nm* Brazil nut
toco *nm* (of cigarette &c) butt
toicinho *nm* lard; bacon
tolda *nf* (of wine) clouding
toldo *nm* (of restaurant &c) awning; sun-blind
toledo *nm* semi-hard cow-ewe-goat cheese
tomar *vt* to to take; to eat
tomatada *nf* tomato-juice
tomate *nm* tomato; **~s-cerejas** cherry tomatoes; **~s recheados** stuffed tomatoes
tomilho *nm* thyme
tona *nf* skin; rind; peel
tonel *nm* vat
tônica *nf* tonic
toniha *nf* sea fish: young tunny
topinambo *nm* Jerusalem artichoke
toque *nm* (of wine) bouquet; nose
toranja (toronja) *nf* grapefruit
torcer *vt* to twist
tornassol *nm* sunflower

torneira *nf* tap; (of cooker) knob; (of barrel) tap

toronja *nf* grapefruit

torpedo *nm* sea fish: crampfish

torra *nf* roasting; toasting

torrada *nf* toast; **~ com manteiga** buttered toast; **~ com queijo derretido** Welsh rarebit (rabbit); **sobre ~** on toast

torrado *a* toasted; roasted; crisp

torrador *nm* toaster; (of coffee &c) roaster

torrão (~ões *pl) nm* (of sugar &c) lump

torrar *vt* to roast; to toast; to grill; to brown

torrefação *nf* roasting; toasting

torrefato (torrefeito) *a* roasted; toasted

torrefator *nm* roaster; toaster

torrefazer *vt* to roast; to toast

torrija *nf* wine-dunked sugared/egged toast; French toast

torta *nf* tart; pie; flan; cake; **~ de camarão** shrimp pie; **~ de chocolate** chocolate tart; **~ de frango** chicken pie; **~ de frutas** fruit tart; **~ de geléia** jam-tart; **~ de limão** key lime pie; **~ de maçã** apple pie; **~ de maçã de massa folhada** apfelstrudel; **~ de nozes** walnut tart; **~ de queijo** cheese pie; **~ de ricota** cheesecake; **~ de rim** kidney pie; **~ salgada** savoury flan

torteira *nf* baking-pan

tortilha *nf* tortilla

tortulho *nm* young mushroom

tostadela *nf* toasting

tostado *a* toasted

tostadura *nf* toasting; roasting

tostar *vt* to toast; to roast

toste *nm* (of salutation) toast; buttered-toast

toucinho (toicinho) *nm* lard; bacon

touro (toiro) *nm* bull

trabalhar *vt* to work; to knead; to beat

trabuco *nm* [Braz] large [cheap] cigar

tracalhaz (tracanaz) *nm* large slice; hunk

traço *nm* [Braz] (of drink) gulp

tradicional *a* traditional

tragacanto *nm* (of food additive) tragacanth

tragar *vt* to swallow; to gulp

trago *nm* gulp

traguear *vt* [Braz] to gulp

traíra *nf* [Braz] freshwater fish: wolf fish, tiger fish, mud characin, traira

trairão *nm* [Braz] freshwater fish: ray-finned characin

trapalhado *a* (of milk) half-curdled

traseira *nf* hind-quarters

trasfega (trasfegadura) (trasfego *nm) nf* decanting

trasfegar *vt* to decant; to pour out

trato *nm* (of food) fare

travessa *nf* platter
treme-treme *nm* [Braz] electric eel
tremelga *nf* sea fish: crampfish
tremido *nm* over-ripe
trempe *nf* trivet
três *nm* (of number) three; **~-irmãos** *nm* (of plant) soapberry variety
trigamilha *nf* maize/wheat bread
trigo *nm* wheat; corn; **~-durázio** durum wheat; **~-de-milagre** mummy wheat; **~-mouro (~ sarraceno)** buckwheat
triguilho *nm* (of wheat) chaff
trinca *nf* [Braz] mouthful
trincado *a* (of plate &c) cracked
trinchante *nm/f* carving knife, carver; serving-dish
trinchar *vt* (of meat) to carve; cut up
trincho *nm* carving/chopping board; serving-dish
tripa *nf* tripe; **~s** chitterlings; **~s à moda do Porto** (of dish) sausage/bean/onion/herb/spiced veal/chicken tripe
tripagem (tripalhada) *nf* tripe butcher
triparia *nf* tripe butcher's
tritíceo *a* wheat
triturar *vt* to grind; to beat
triunfo *nm* (of banqueting table) centre-piece
trivial *nm* [Braz] plain cooking
trocados *nmpl* small change; (of gratuity) tip
troco *nm* (of coins) small change
trolha *nf* (of sausage-making) tube
tromba-de-elefante *nf* agave variety
tronchuda *nf* cabbage variety
trufa (túbera) *nf* (of mushroom) truffle
trufar *vt* (of mushroom) to truffle
trufeiro *nm* truffle-seller
truque *nm* (of cooking method) hint
truta *nf* freshwater fish: trout; **~-arco-íris** rainbow trout; **~-commum** brown trout; **~das-fontes** char; **~ defumado** smoked trout; **~-de-lago** lake trout; **~-salmoneja** sea trout
tubarana (tabarana) (dourado-branco) *nf* [Chile] freshwater fish: tabarana
tubarão *nm* sea fish: shark; dogfish
tubo *nm* (of cigarettes) holder
tucumã *nf* [Braz] (of fruit) tucuma; fresh-water turtle
tucunare *nm* [Braz] freshwater fish: peacock bass
tucupi *nm* cassava-pepper dressing
tufas grelhadas *nfpl* grilled squid
tumbança *nf* sweet cashew-nut dish

tungar *vt* [Braz] to dunk
tupinambo (tupinambor) *nm* [Braz] Jerusalem artichoke
turíngia *nf* orange variety
túrnepo *nm* turnip variety; **~-brancho** common turnip
tururi *nm* Brazil nut
tutano *nm* (of bone) marrow
tutu *nm* cassava/bean/bacon dish
tuvira *nf* [Braz] freshwater fish: eel

U

uariquina *nf* [Braz] red pepper variety
ubarana (uborana) (abarana) *nf* [Braz] sea fish: ladyfish
uca *nf* brandy
uchão *nm* butler; steward
ueua (saicanga) (peixe-cachorro) *nf* [Braz] freshwater fish: saicanga
uísque *nm* whisky; whiskey; **~ com soda** whisky and soda
uisqueria *nf* [Braz] whisky bar
um (uma *nf) nm* (of number) one
umbrela (umbela) *nf* umbrella
unha *nf* (of crustacean) claw; (of pig) trotter
untar *vt* to grease
unto *nm* lard; fat; oil
untuoso *a* greasy; fatty
urso *nm* bear
urtiga *nf* stinging-nettle
uru *nm* partridge
utensílio *nm* utensil; **~s de cozinha** kitchen utensils; kitchenware
uva *nf* grape; **bago de ~** grape; **~-dos-bosques** blueberry; **~-brava** sorrel; **cacho de ~s** bunch of grapes; **~-espim** barberry;**~ ~-do-monte** bilberry; **~-passa** raisin; plum; **semente de ~** grape pip; **~-de-urso (~-ursina)** bearberry
uvada *nf* grape jam

V

vaca *nf* cow; beef
vacância (vacatura) *nf* vacancy
vacante *a* vacant; free
vacum *a* bovine
vácuo *nm* vacuum
vagão *nm* railway carriage; **~ restaurante** dining-car
vagem *nf* French bean; kidney bean; haricot bean; snap-bean; pod; **~ de baunilha** vanilla
valor nutritivo *nm* food-value
vapor *nm* steam
vaporar *vt* to steam
vaquilhona (vaquinha) *nf* young cow; heifer
vara *nf* stick; **~ de arame** wire beater/whisk
varinha *nf* small beater
varrão *nm* boar
varredouro (varredoira) *nm*

oven-brush
varredura *nf* (of food) scraps
vasculho *nm* (of oven) brush
vasilha *nf* jug; dish; container; barrel
vaso *nm* bowl; jar; vase; urn
vassouro (vassoiro) *nf* oven-brush
vatapá *nm* (of dish) meat/fish/ coconut-milk/dried-shrimp/ chili/cassava
vazamento (vazadura) *nm* (of liquid) leakage; spilling
vazar *vt* to spill; to empty; to pour out; to drink
vazio *a* empty
veação *nf* game; venison
veada *nf* (of deer) hind
veado *nm* red deer
veda *nf* (of game) close season
vedação *nf* prohibition
vedado *a* prohibited
vegetal *nm* vegetable; *a* **gordura ~** vegetable fat
vegetariano *nm/a* vegetarian; **regime ~** vegetarian diet
vegetarista *nm/f* vegetarian
vegetável *a* vegetable
vela *nf* candle
velho *a* (of vintage &c) old
vencimento *nm* sell-by date
venda *nf* sale; grocery
vendedor *nm* seller
vendedouro (vendedoiro) *nm* market-place
vendeiro *nm* innkeeper; grocer
venera *nf* scallop shell
veneziana *nf* Venetian blind; shutter
venezolano (venezuelano) *nm* Venezuelan
ventre *nm* stomach
ventrícola *a* good-food-appreciating
verão *nm* summer
verbena *nf* verbena
verdasco *nm* sour wine
verde *nm* (of herbal tea) maté; *a* green
verdear *vt* to drink maté
verdelho *nm* (of wine) medium-dry madeira
verdete *nm* grape variety
verdoso (verdoengo) (verdolengo) *a* unripe
verdura *nf* vegetables; greens; (of meat dish ingredients) à la mode
verdureiro (verduleiro [Braz]) *nm* greengrocer
vergamota *nf* [Braz] tangerine; manderin
vergel *nm* garden; orchard
vermelho *nm* red; **~ (~-cioba)** sea fish: southern red snapper
versar *vt* to turn; to decant
vesco *a* edible
véspera *nf* afternoon; evening
vestiário *nm* cloakroom
vestido de baile *nm* evening-dress
vez *nf* time; occasion
videira *nf* grape-vine
Vidigueira *nm* Alentejo vineyard

vidraria *nf* glassware
vidro *nm* glass; bottle; **~ de cristal** crystal glass; **~ lapidado** cut-glass
vieira *nf* scallop
vináceo *a* (of ingredient) wined
vinagrar (avinagrar) *vt* to vinegar
vinagre *nm* vinegar; **em ~** pickled; **~ balsâmico** balsamic vinegar
vinagreira *nf* vinegar bottle/ cruet
vinagreta *nf* vinaigrette
vindima (vindimadura) *nf* vintage
vindimado *a* (of grapes) harvest
vindimo *a* vintage
vinha *nf* vineyard; vine; **~-d'alhos** vinegar/garlic/pepper marinade
vinhaça *nf* plonk
vinhaço *nm* (of wine-making) grape-skins
vinhal *nm* vineyard; grape variety
vinhão *nm* full-bodied wine; grape variety
vinhataria *nf* viticulture
vinhateiro *nm* wine-grower
vinhedo *nm* vineyard
vinhete *nm* light wine
vinho *nm* wine; **adega de ~** wine cellar; **barril de** wine cask; **~ branco** white wine; **~ branco do Reno** hock; **casa de ~s** wine merchant's; **copo de ~** glass of wine; **copo para ~** wine glass; **~ doce** sweet wine; **~ espumante** sparkling wine; **~ de frutas** verjuice; **~ de gengibre** ginger-wine; **~ licoroso** fortified wine; **~ de maçã** cider; **~ de mesa** table wine; **~ moscatel** muscatel; **~ de palma** palm wine; **~ do Porto** port; **provador de ~** wine-taster; **~ do Reno** Rhine wine; **~ rosado** rosé wine; **~ seco** dry wine; **~ tinto** red wine; claret; **~ verde** green slightly-fizzy wine
vinhoca *nf* plonk
vinícola *a* wine-growing
vinicultura *nf* viniculture
viradinho (virado) *nm* [Braz] egg/beans dish
virgem *a* (of olive oil) virgin
virgínia *nf* (of tobacco) Virginia
víscera *nf* (of fish &c) guts
viscerado *a* (of fish) gutted; cleaned
visco *nm* mistletoe
visita *nf* visit; visitor
visitante *nm/f* visitor; **~ não convidado** gate-crasher; **livro dos ~** visitors' book
vitamina *nf* vitamin
vitela *nf* calf; veal; **~ à milanesa** veal escalope; **~ assado** roast veal
vitelino *a* (of egg) yolk
viticultura *nf* viticulture
vitivinícola *a* wine-growing